Tracing Art

Beautiful World

Tracing Art

Beautiful World

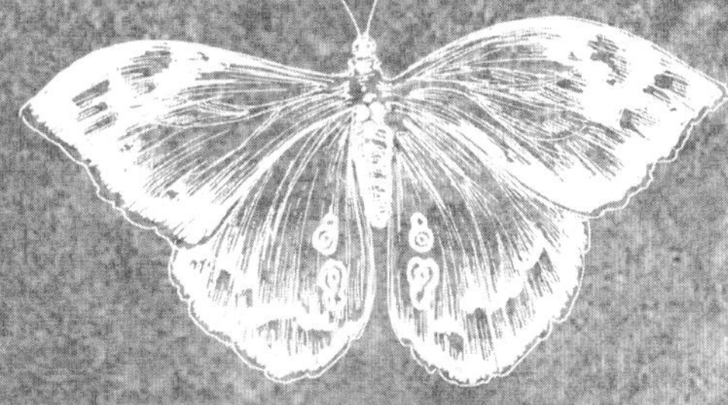

Over 40 beautiful world designs to ink into a charming artwork

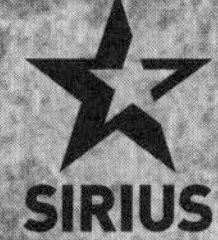

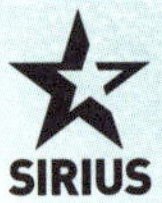

This edition published in 2026 by Sirius Publishing, a division of Arcturus Publishing Limited,
26/27 Bickels Yard, 151–153 Bermondsey Street,
London SE1 3HA

ISBN: 978-1-3988-6229-6
CH013237NT
Supplier 29, Date 1225, PI00011349

Printed in China

Created for children 12+

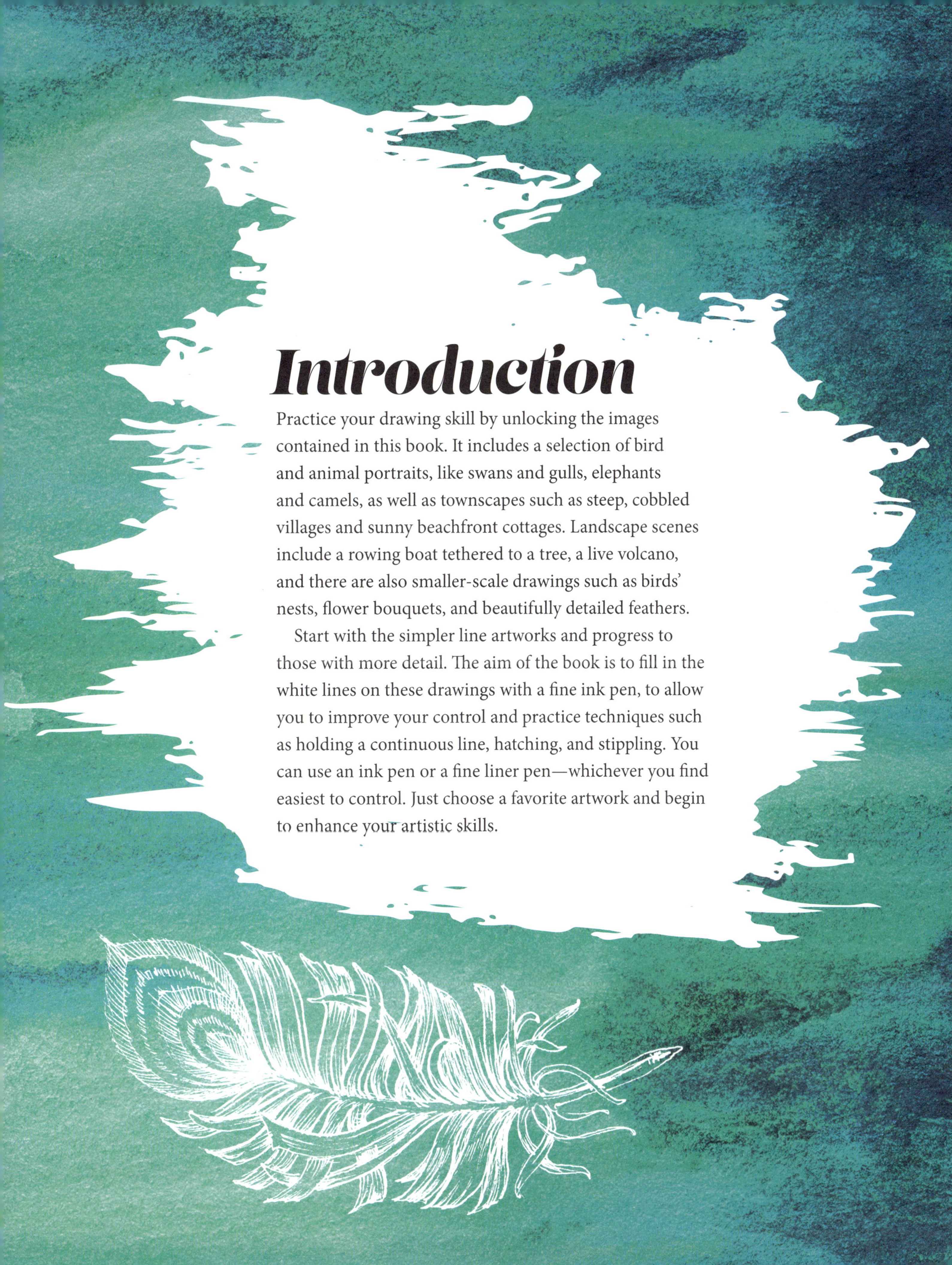

Introduction

Practice your drawing skill by unlocking the images contained in this book. It includes a selection of bird and animal portraits, like swans and gulls, elephants and camels, as well as townscapes such as steep, cobbled villages and sunny beachfront cottages. Landscape scenes include a rowing boat tethered to a tree, a live volcano, and there are also smaller-scale drawings such as birds' nests, flower bouquets, and beautifully detailed feathers.

Start with the simpler line artworks and progress to those with more detail. The aim of the book is to fill in the white lines on these drawings with a fine ink pen, to allow you to improve your control and practice techniques such as holding a continuous line, hatching, and stippling. You can use an ink pen or a fine liner pen—whichever you find easiest to control. Just choose a favorite artwork and begin to enhance your artistic skills.

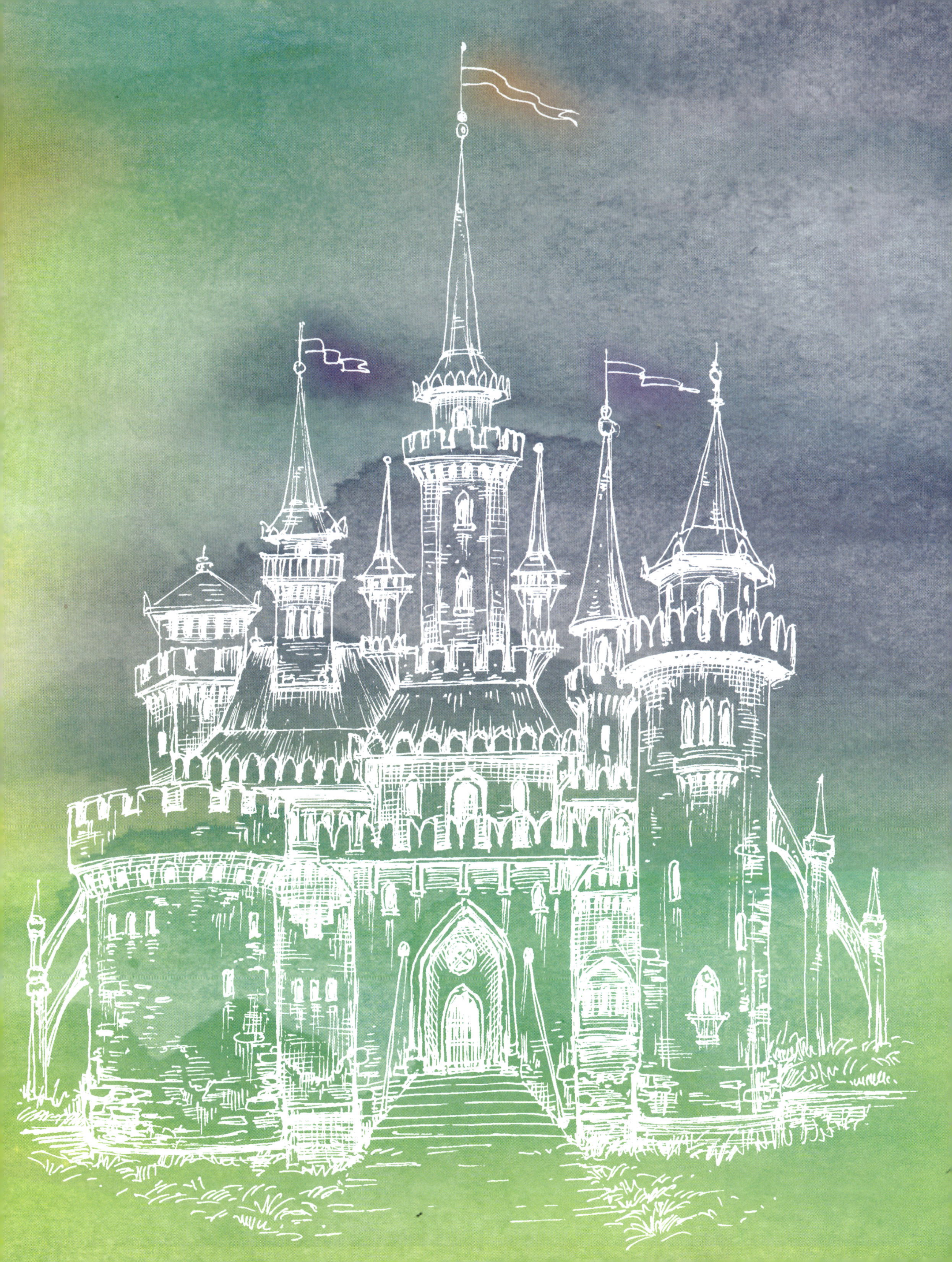

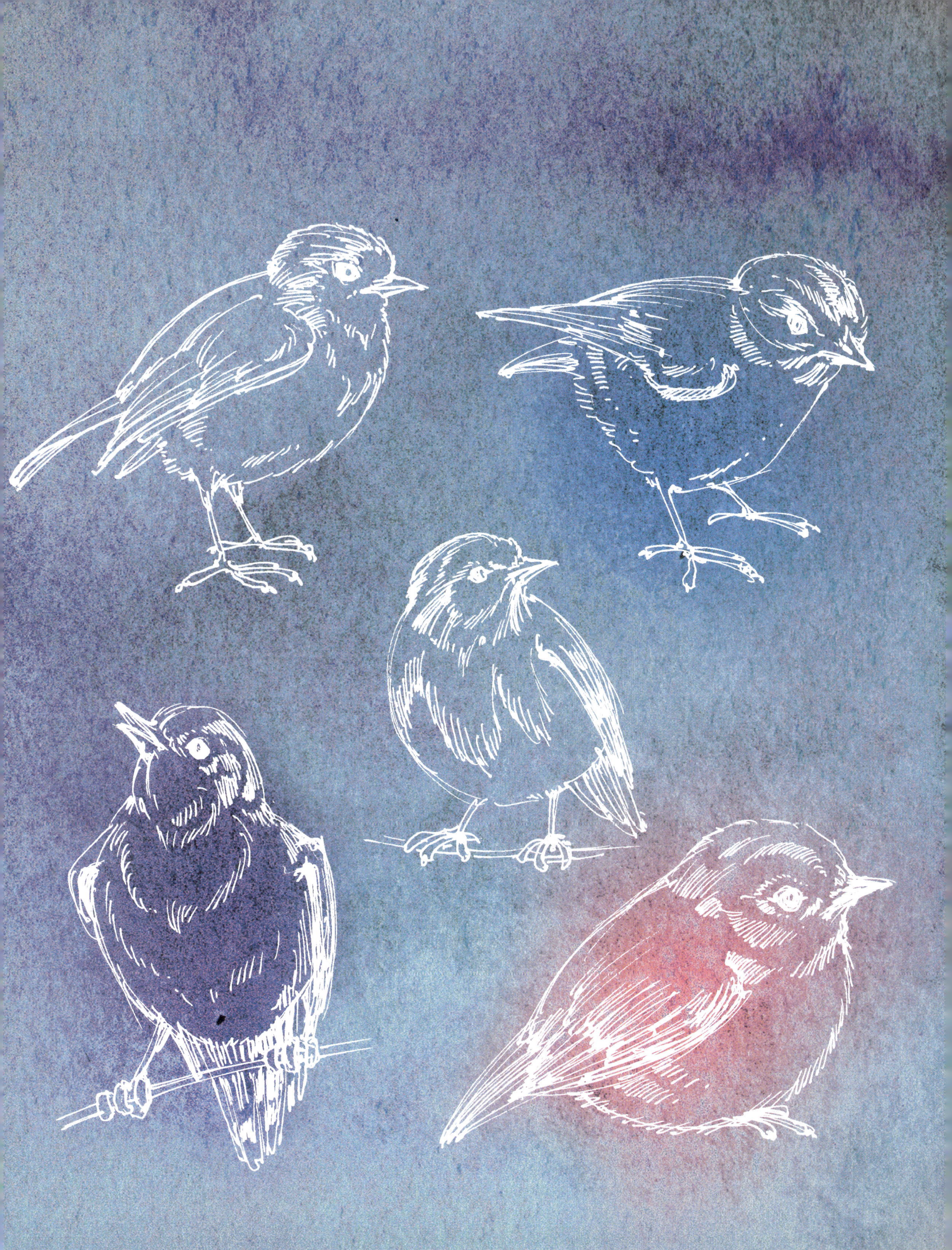

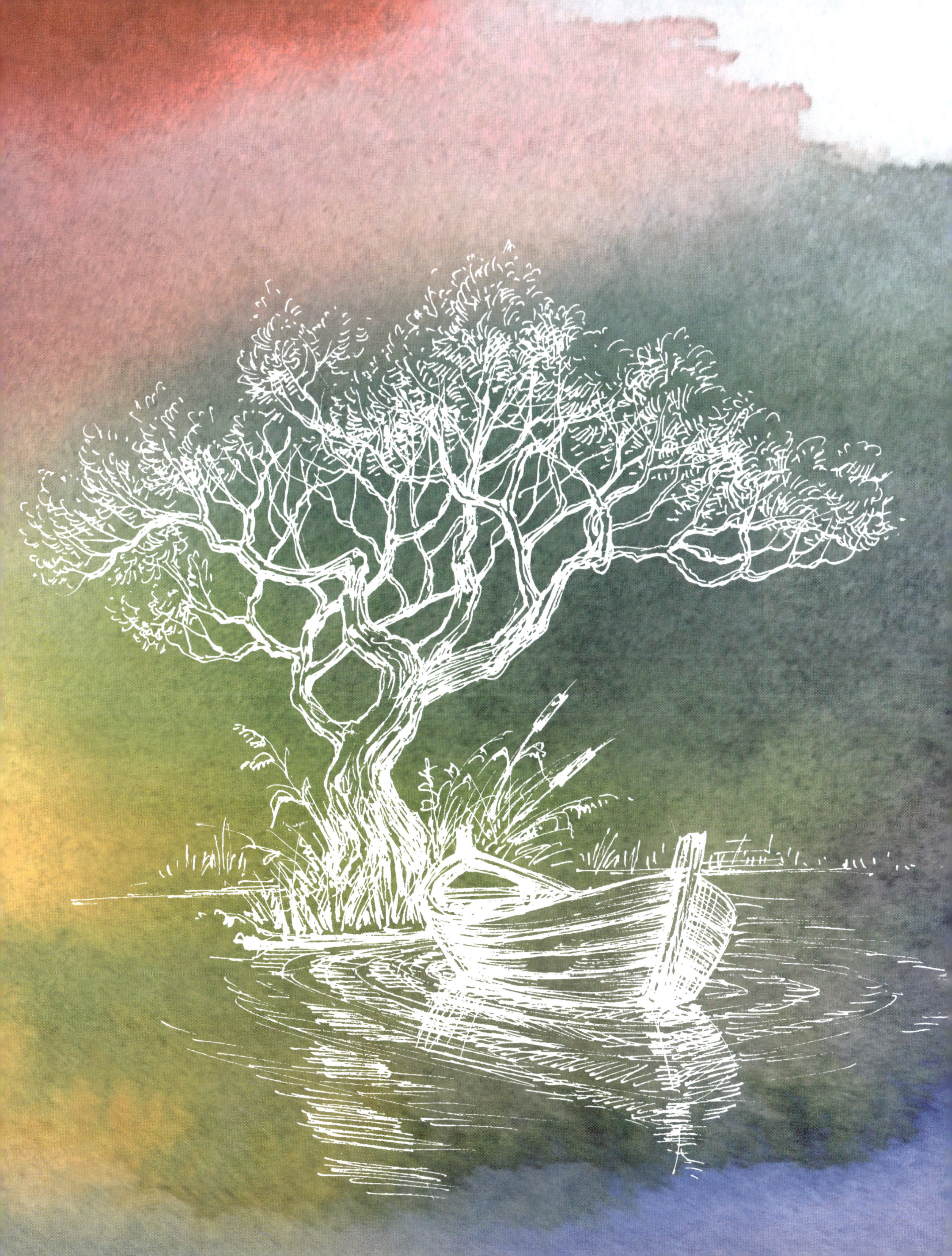

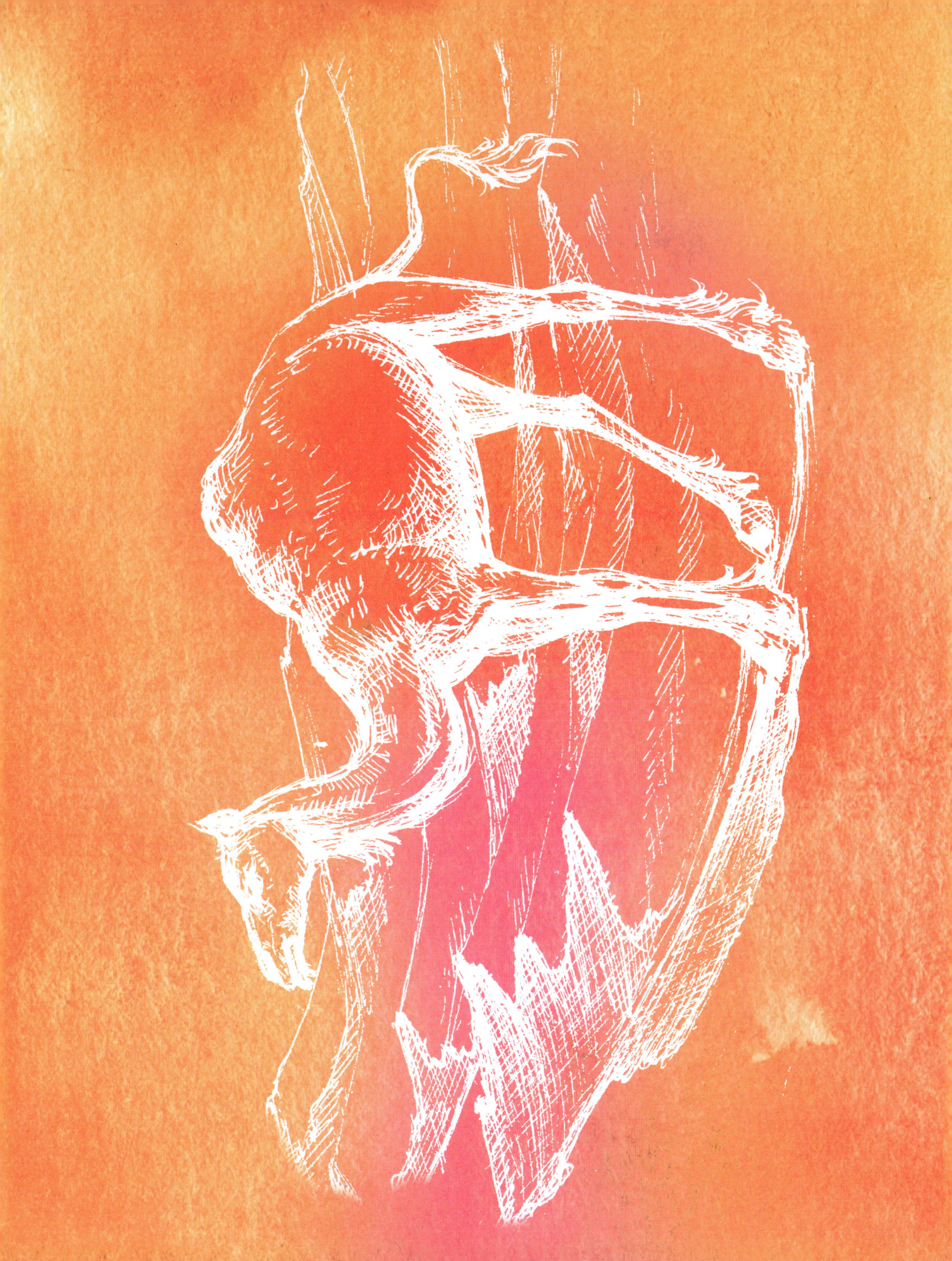

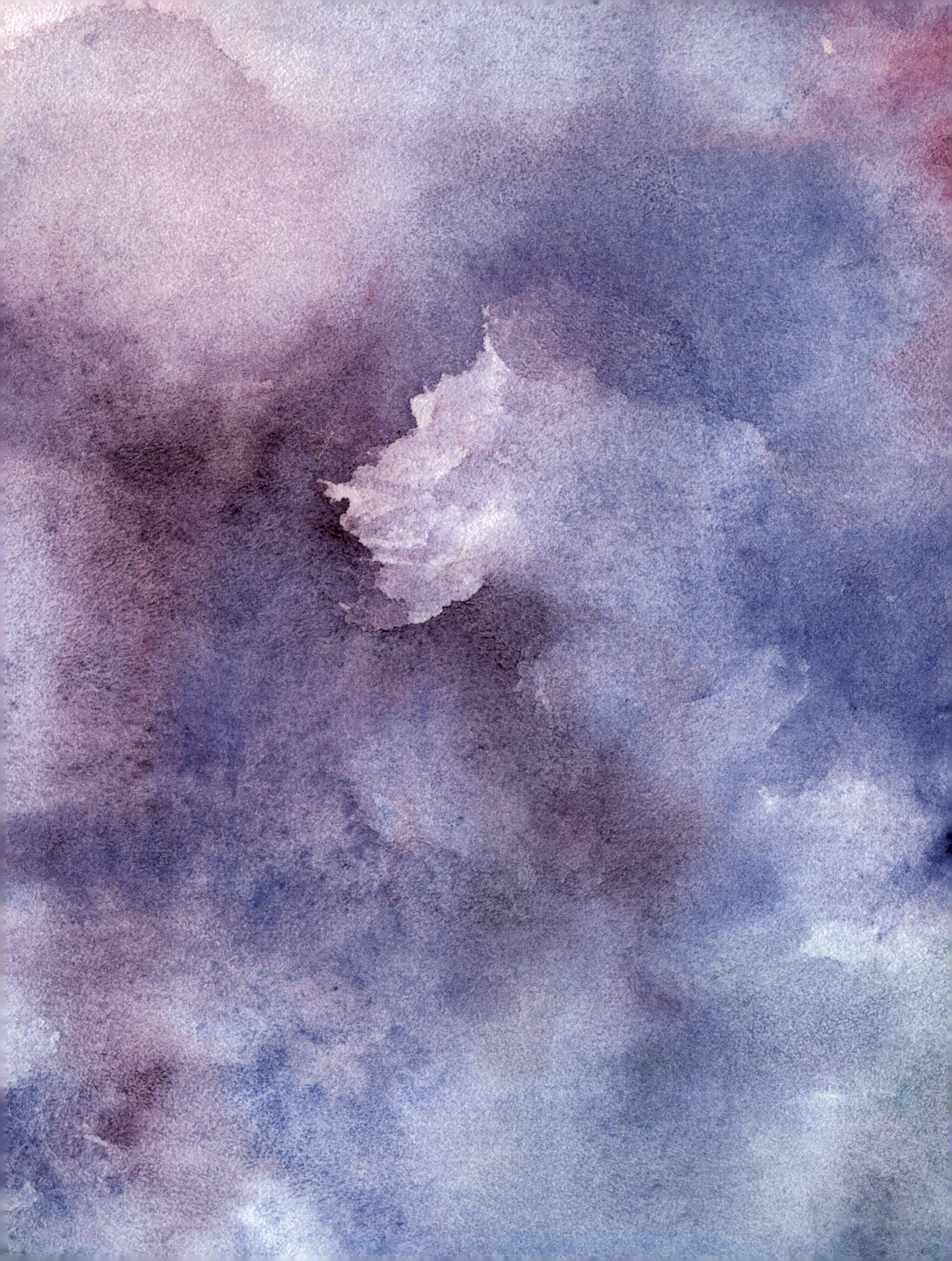

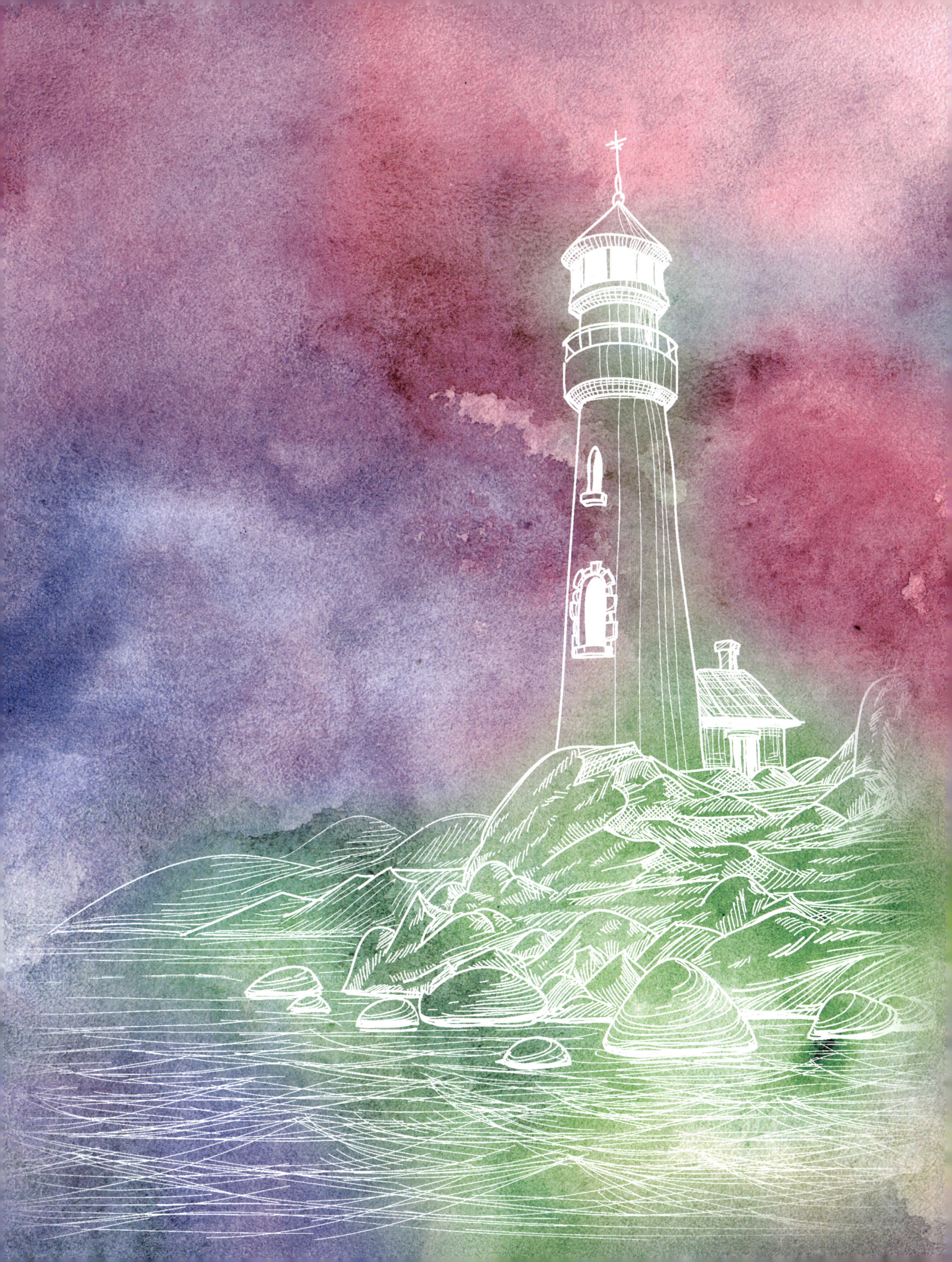

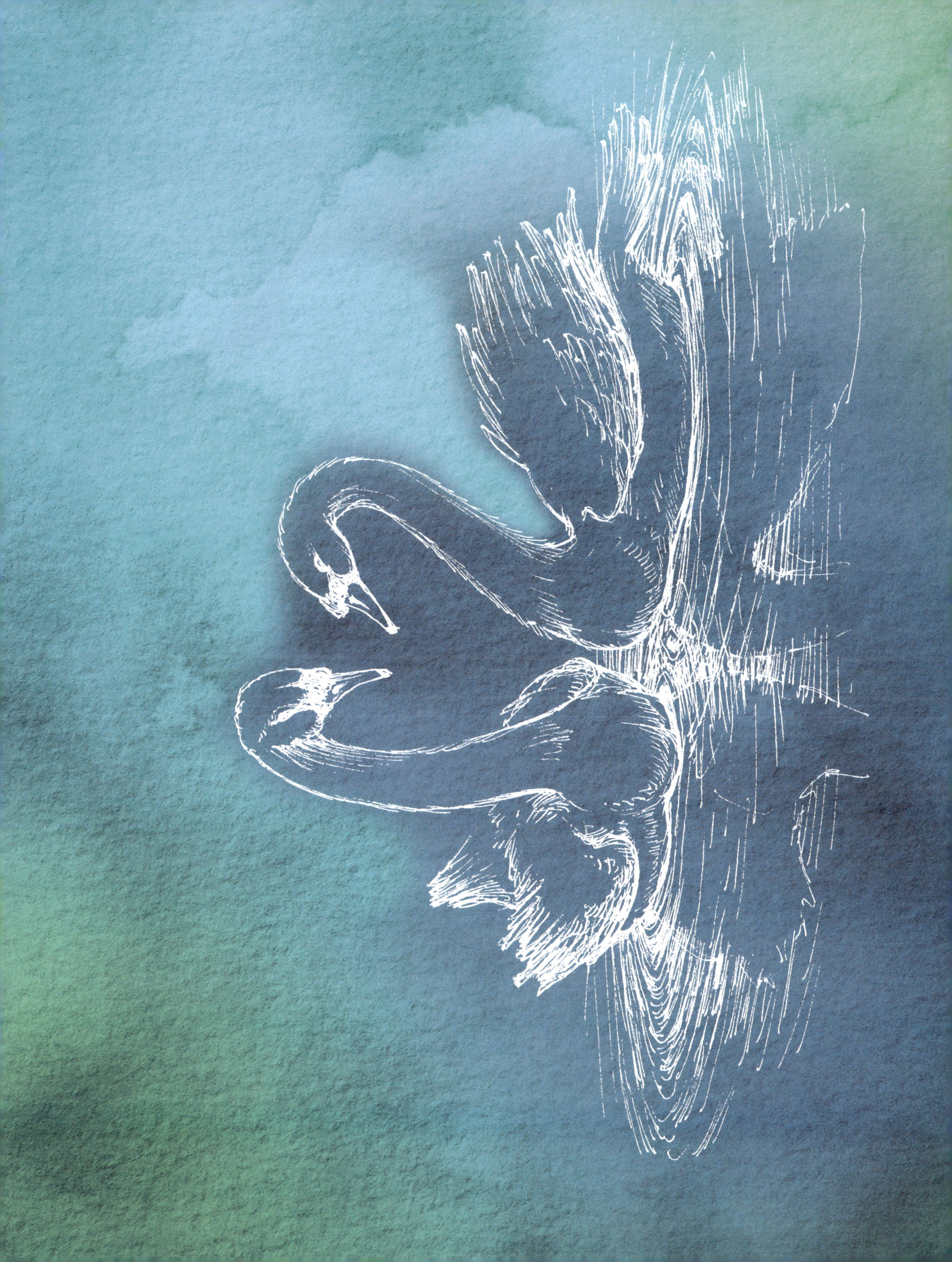

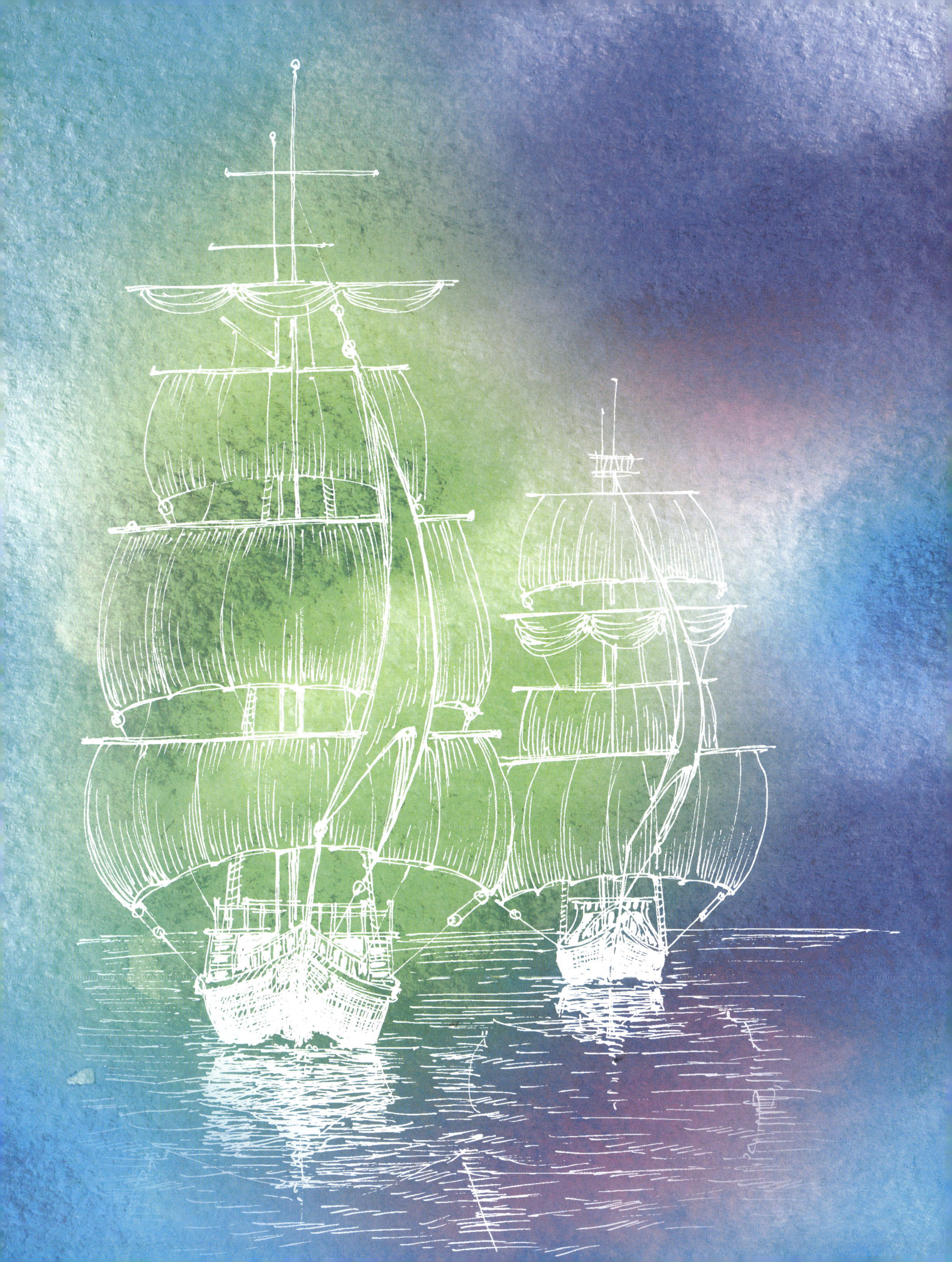

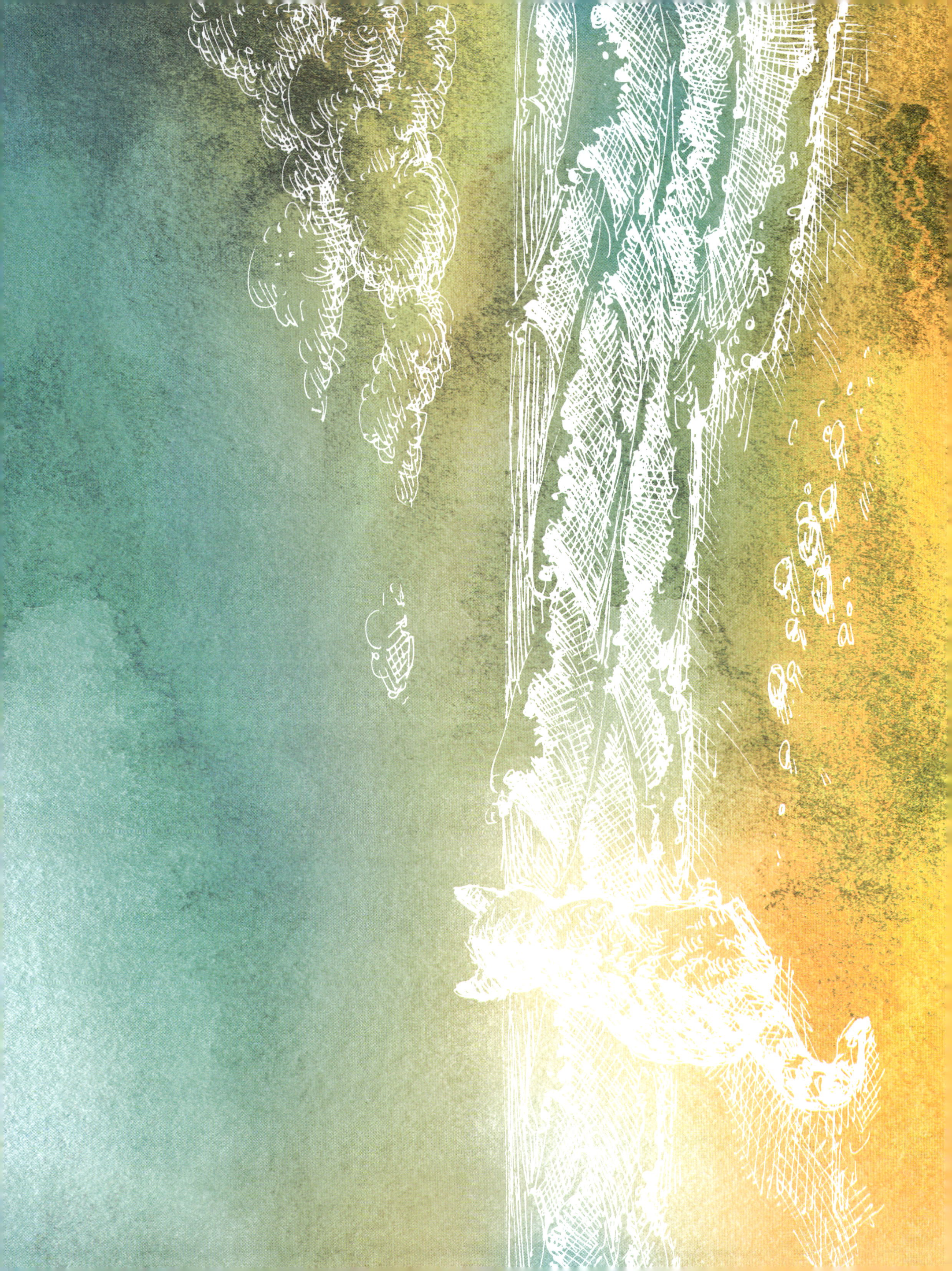

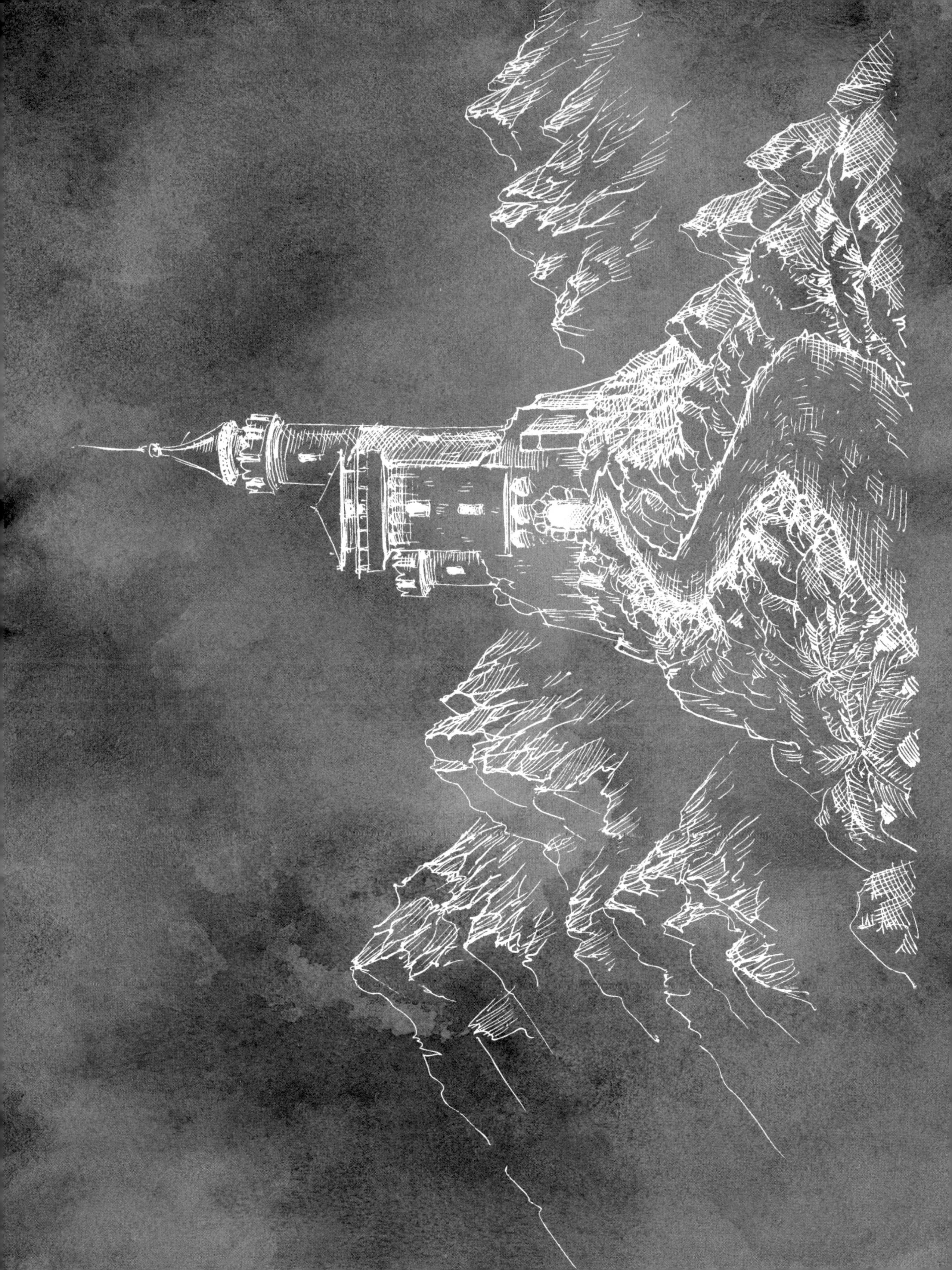

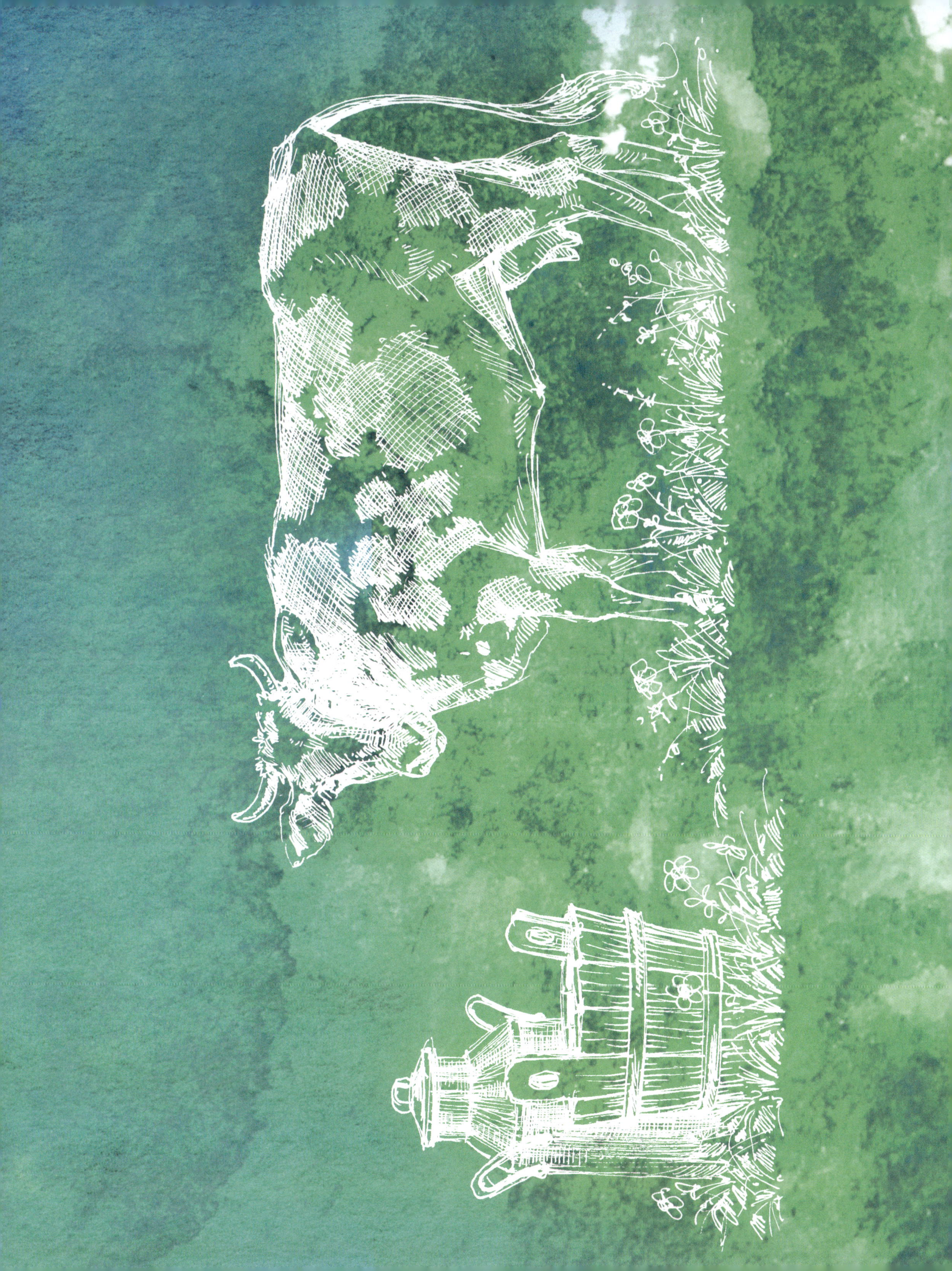

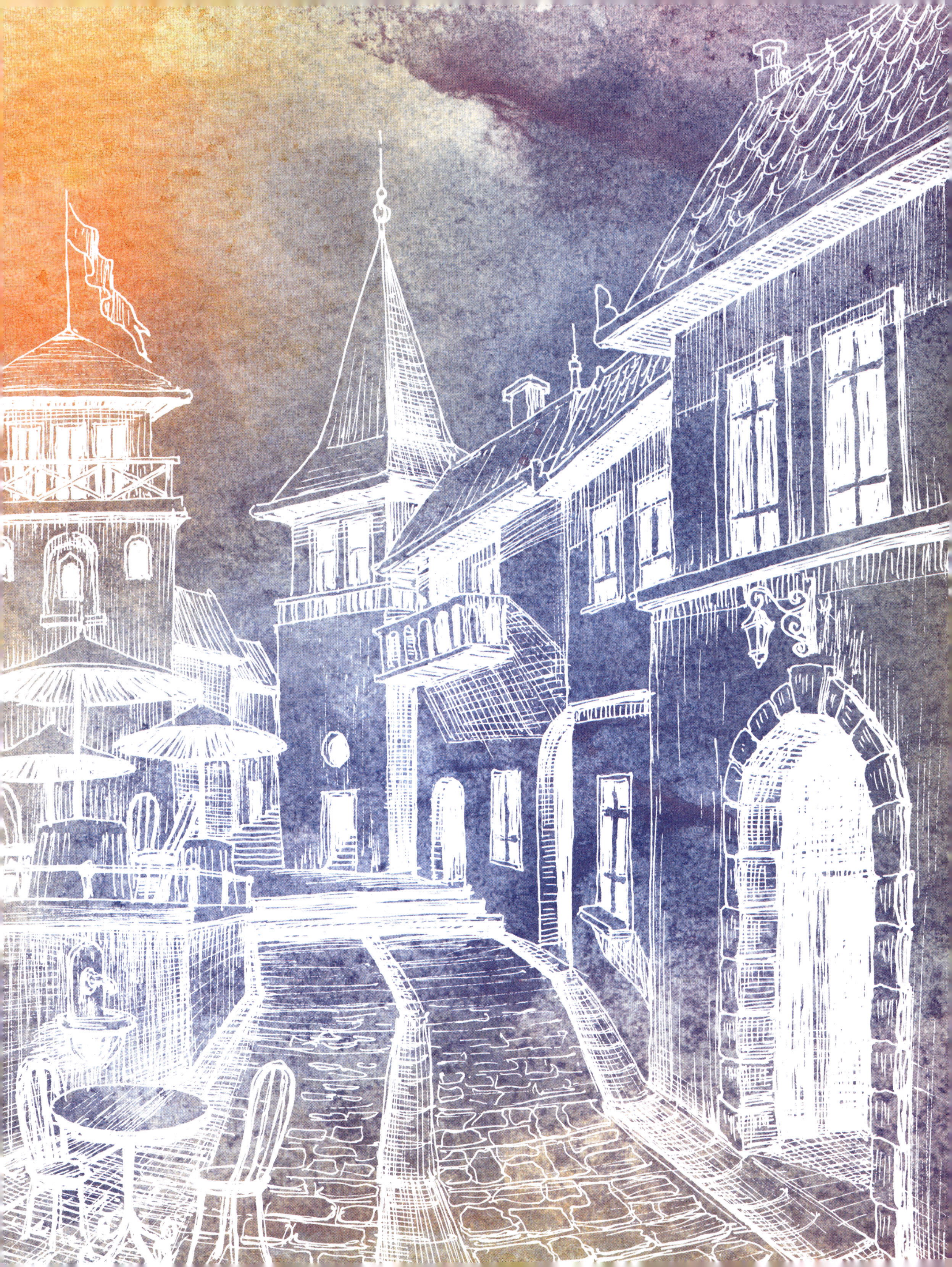

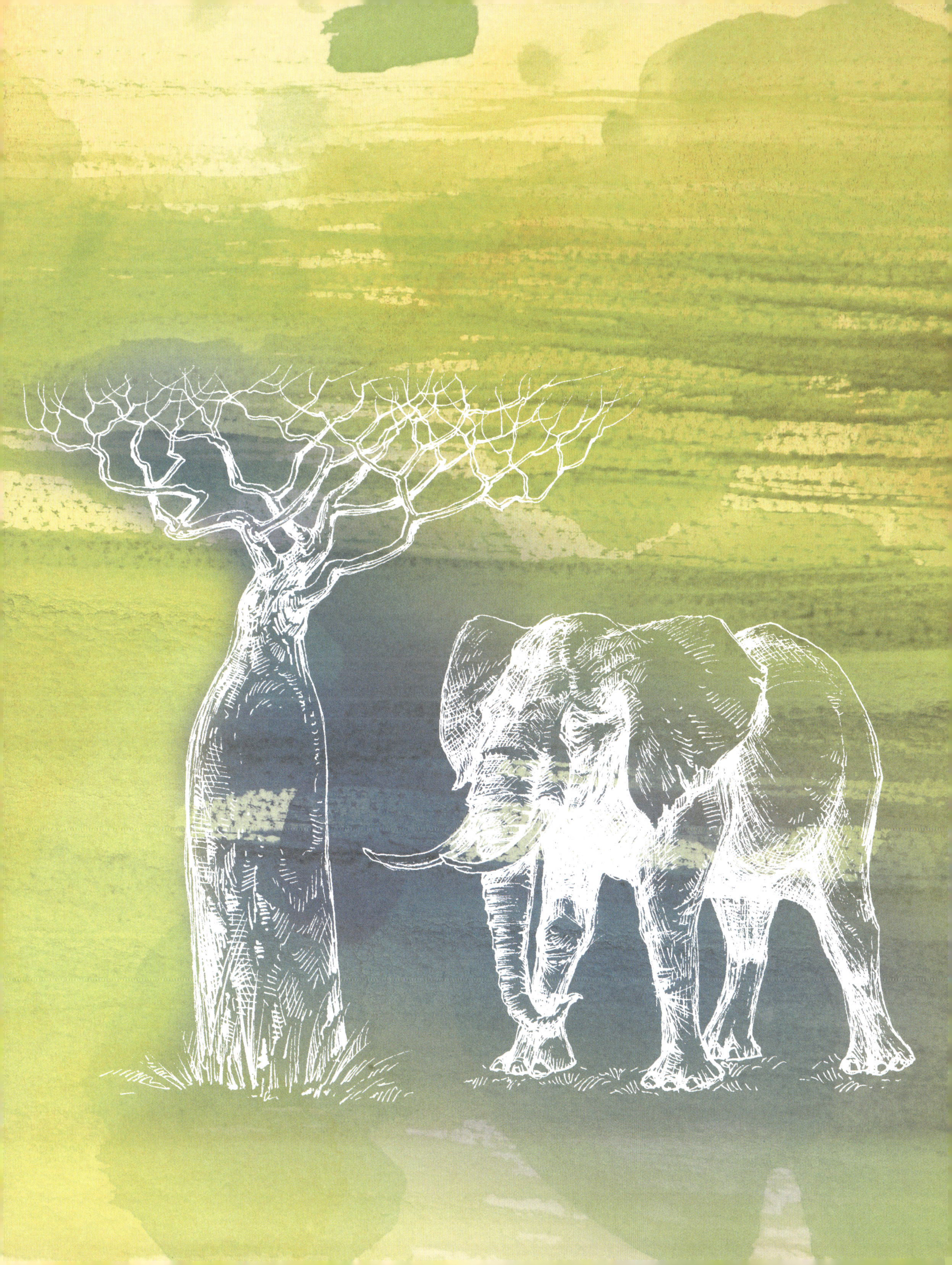

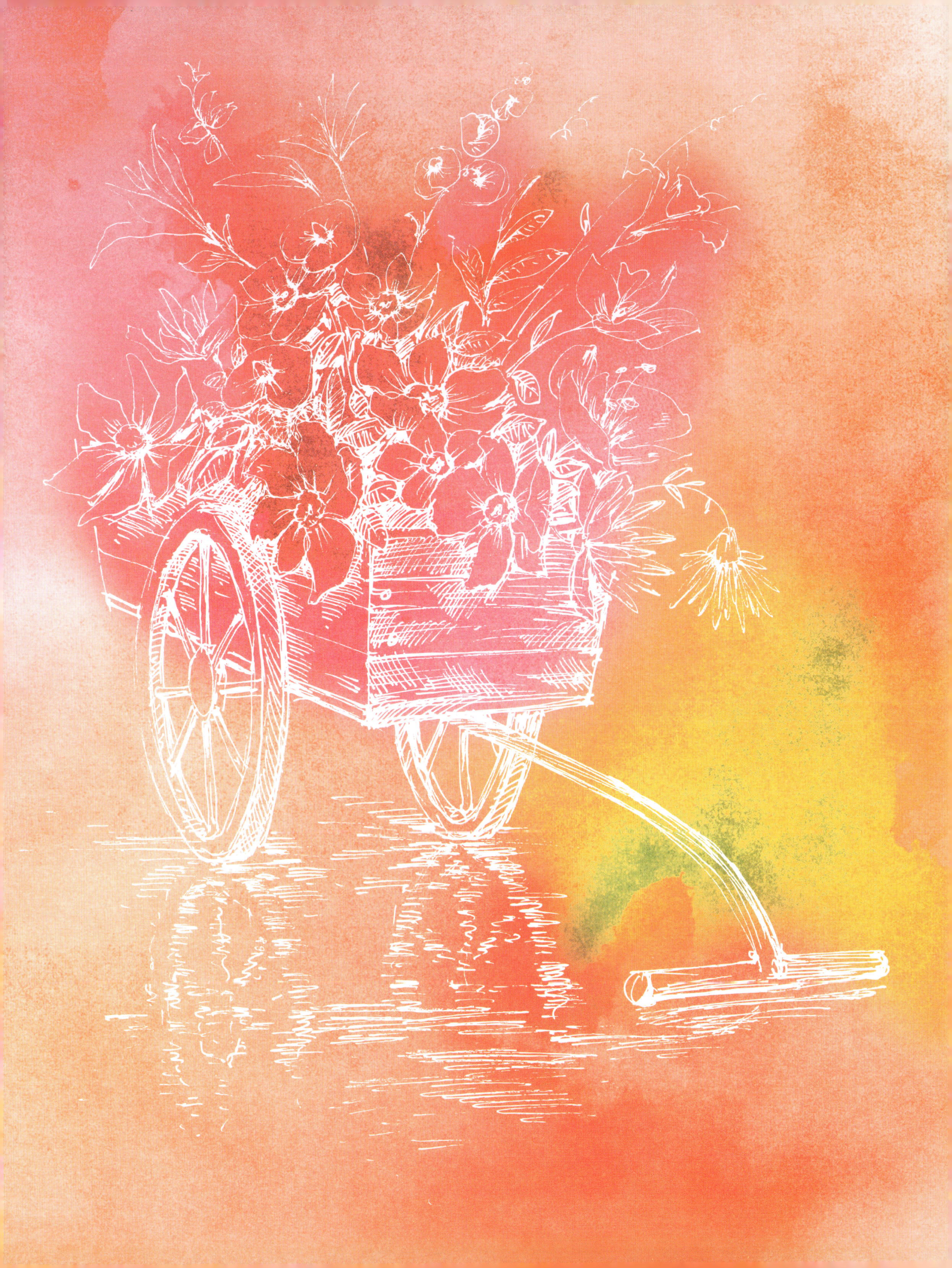

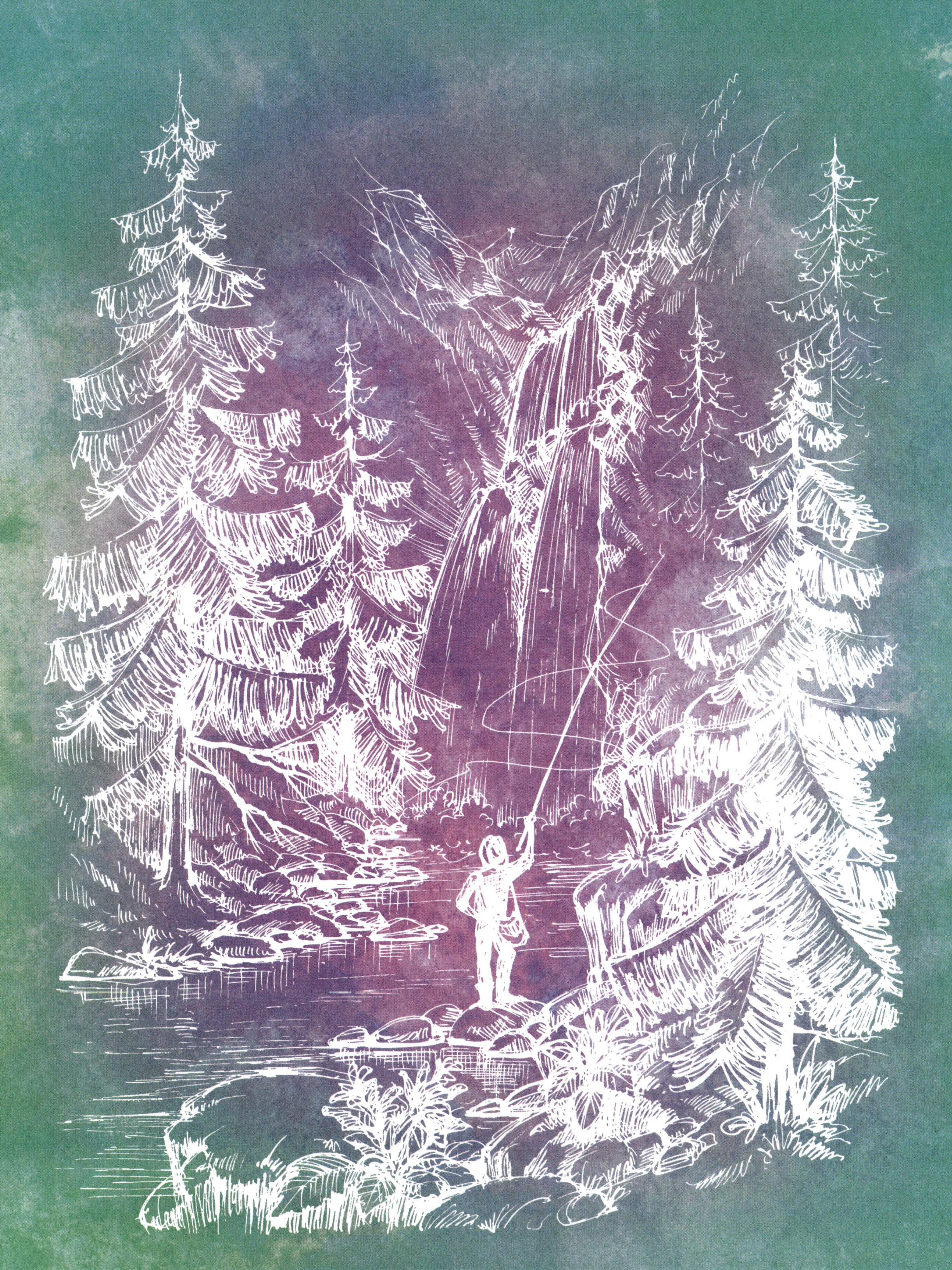

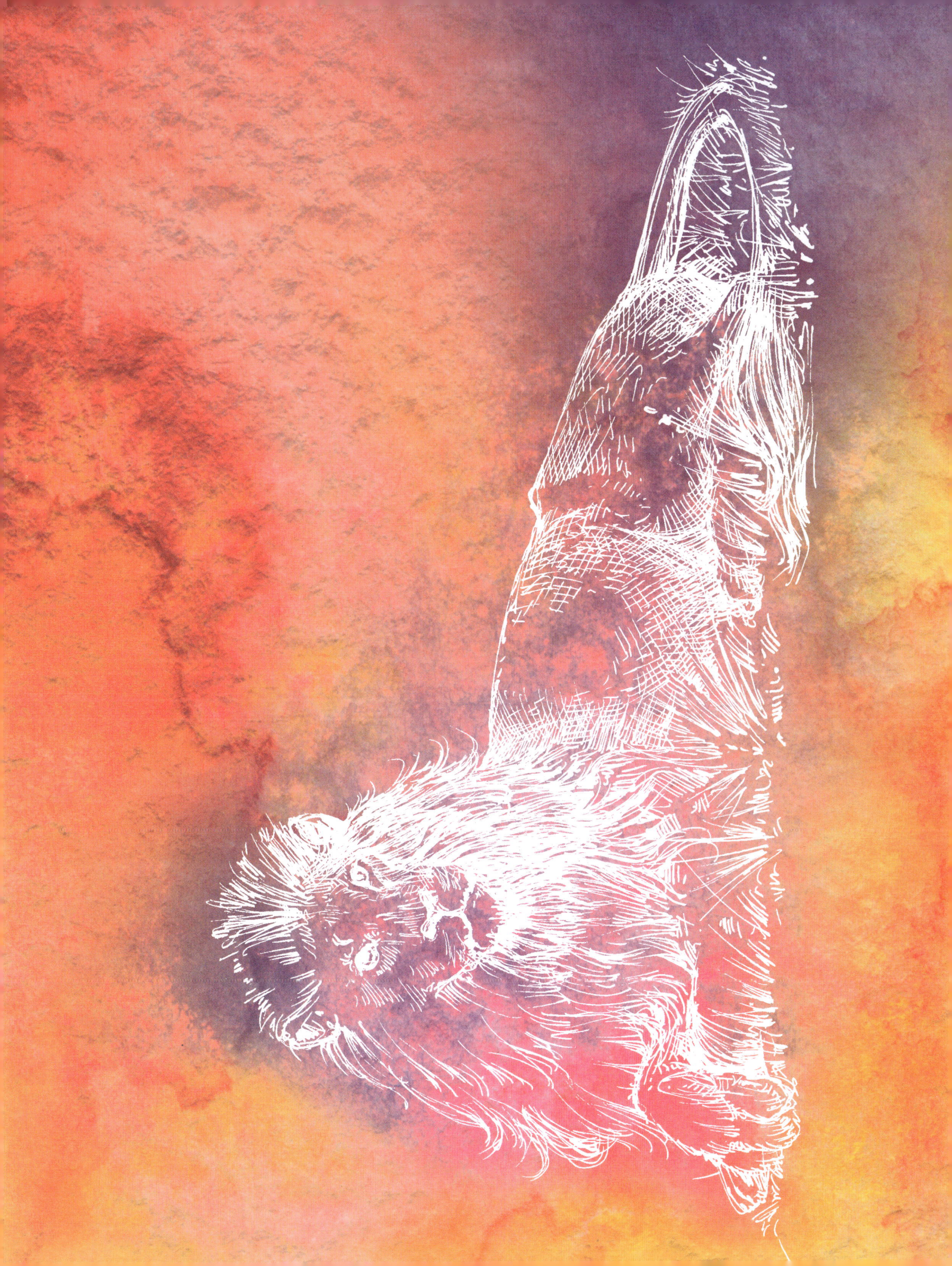

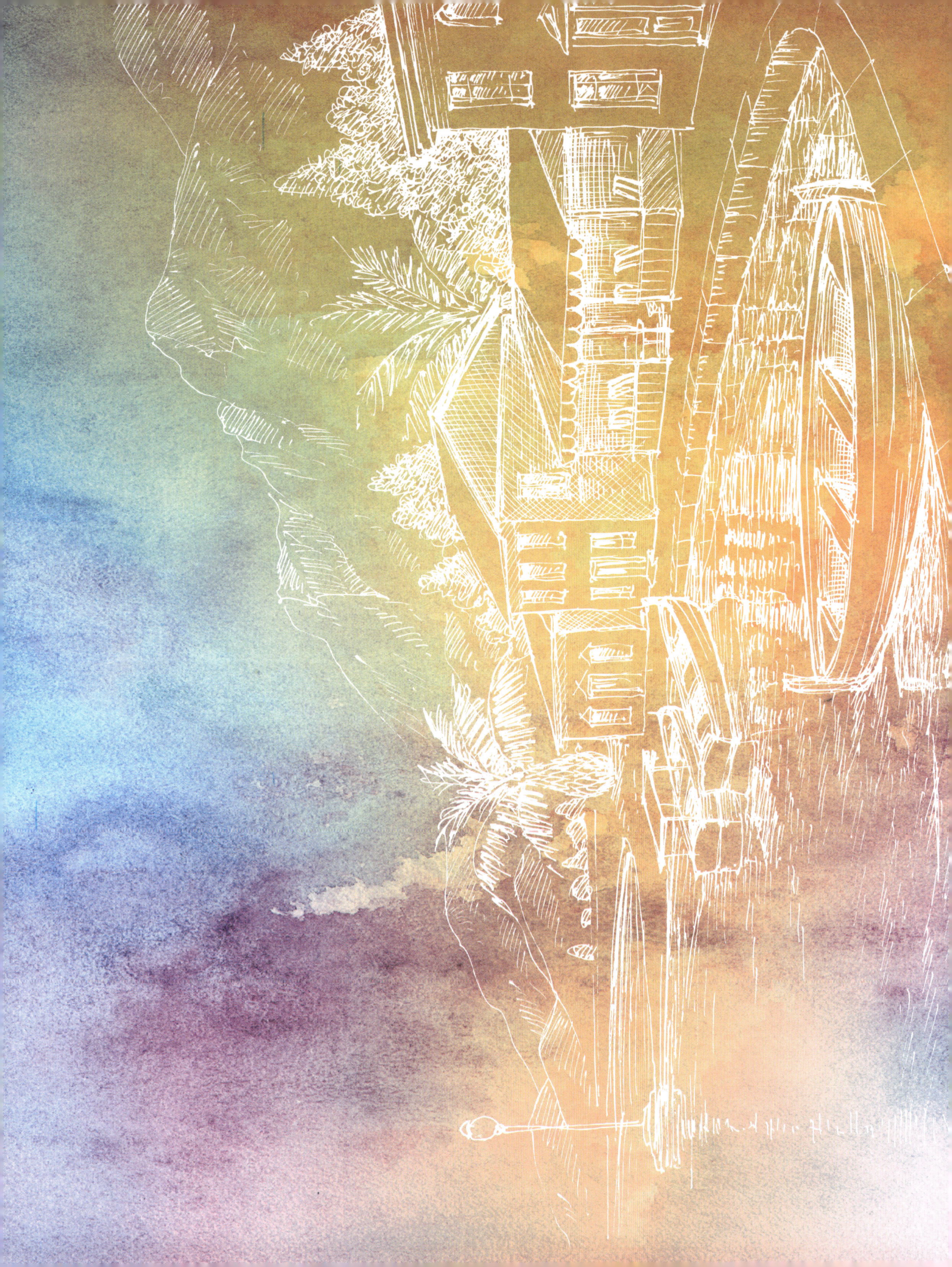

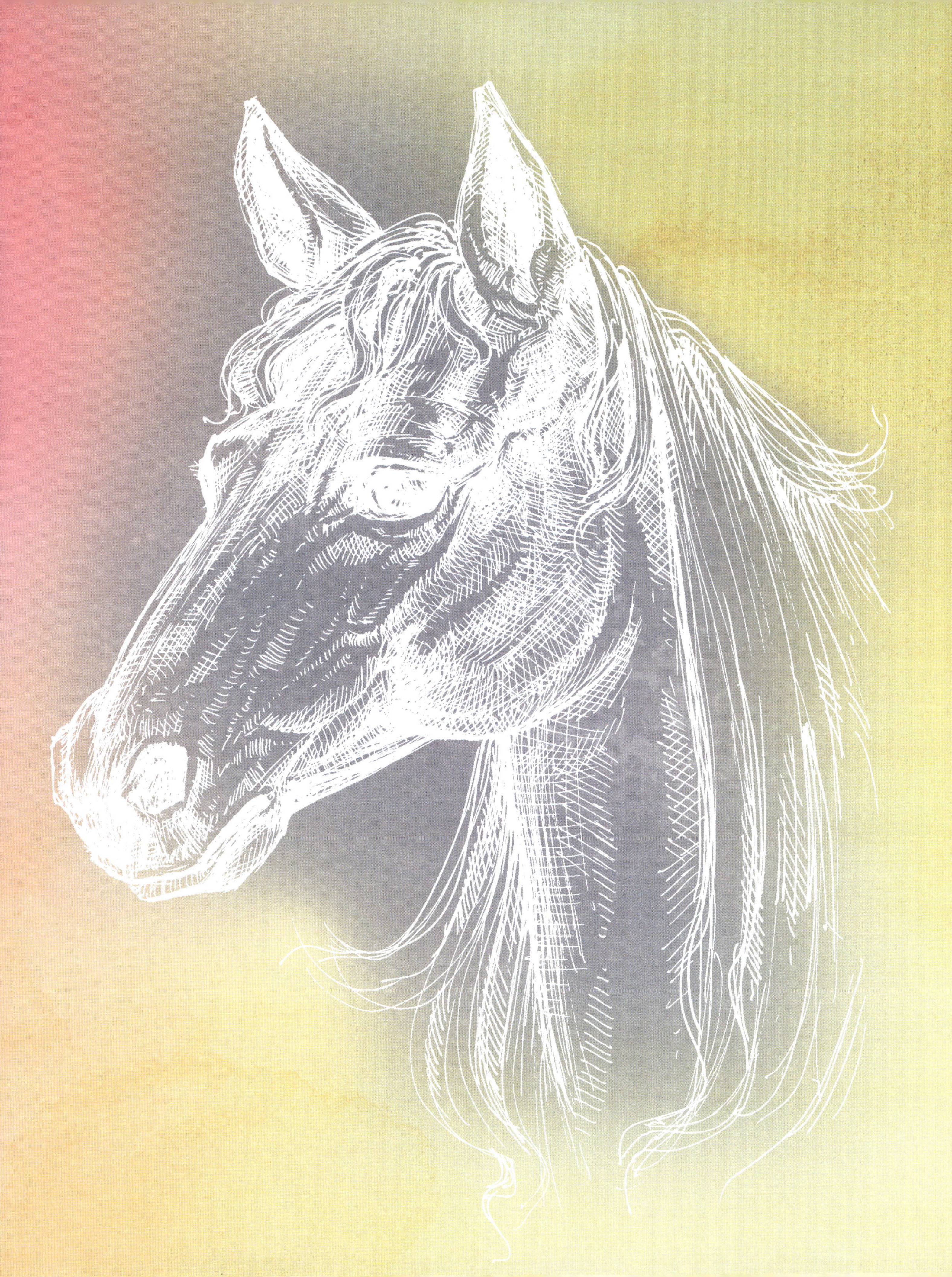

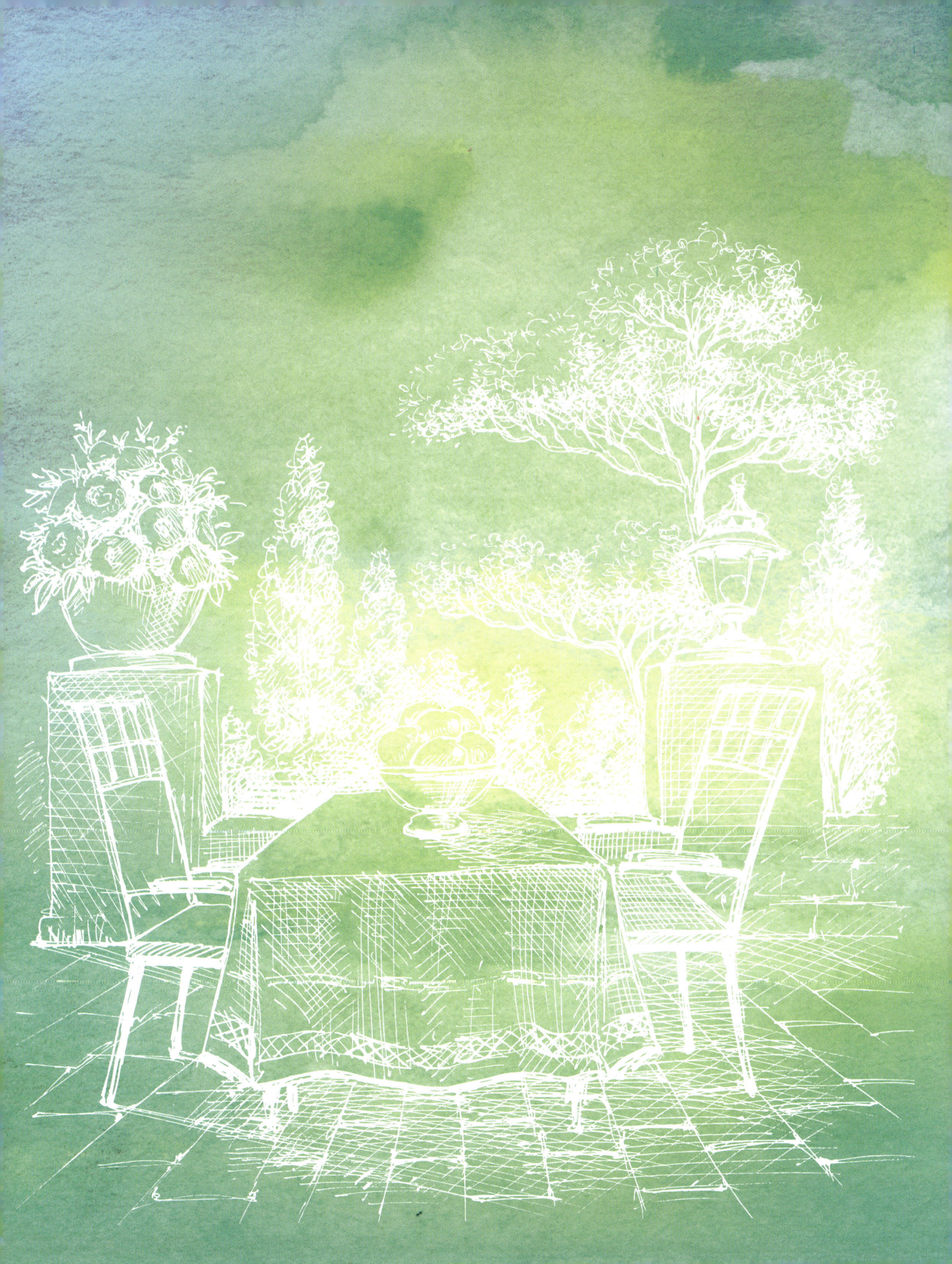

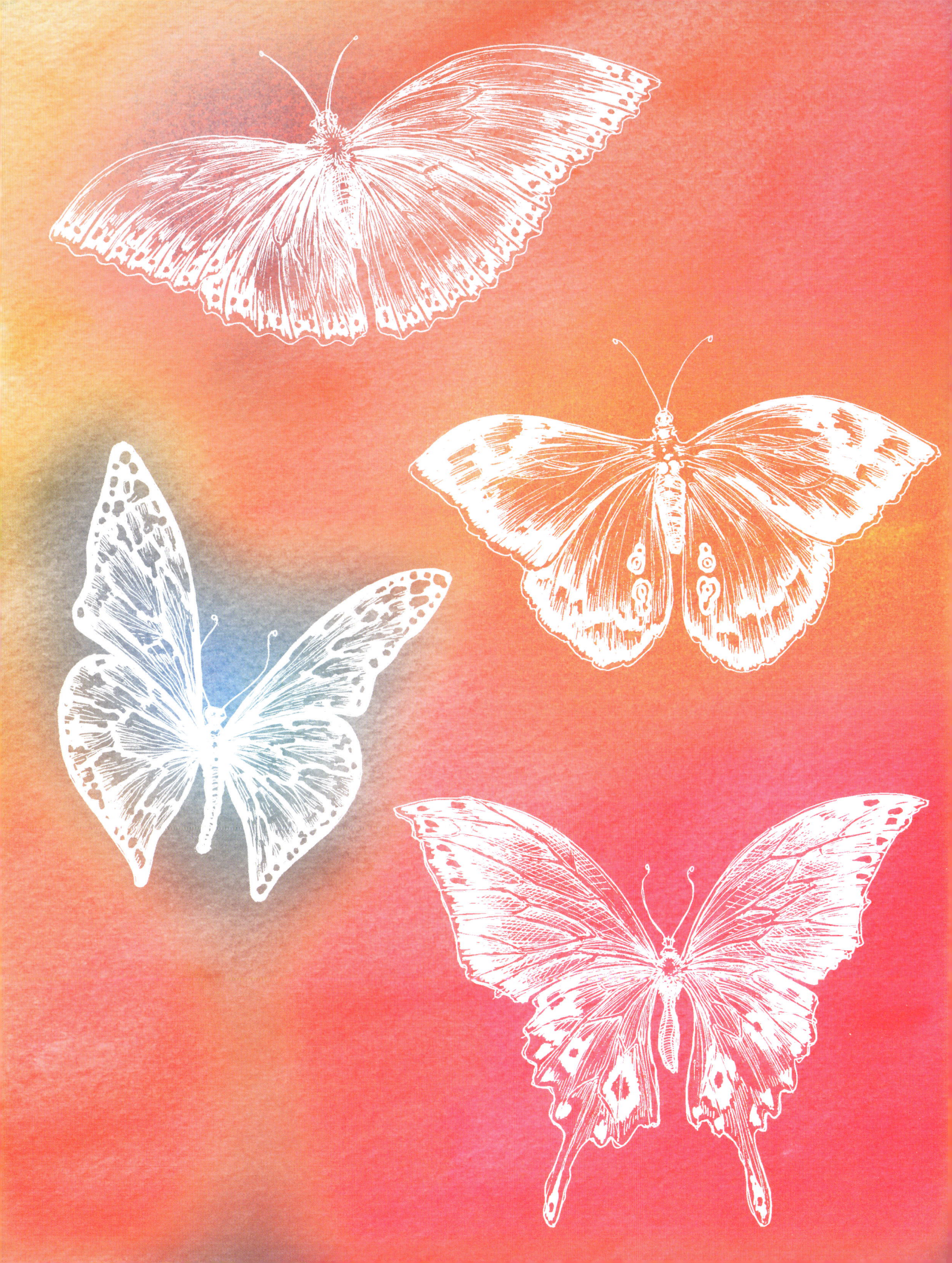

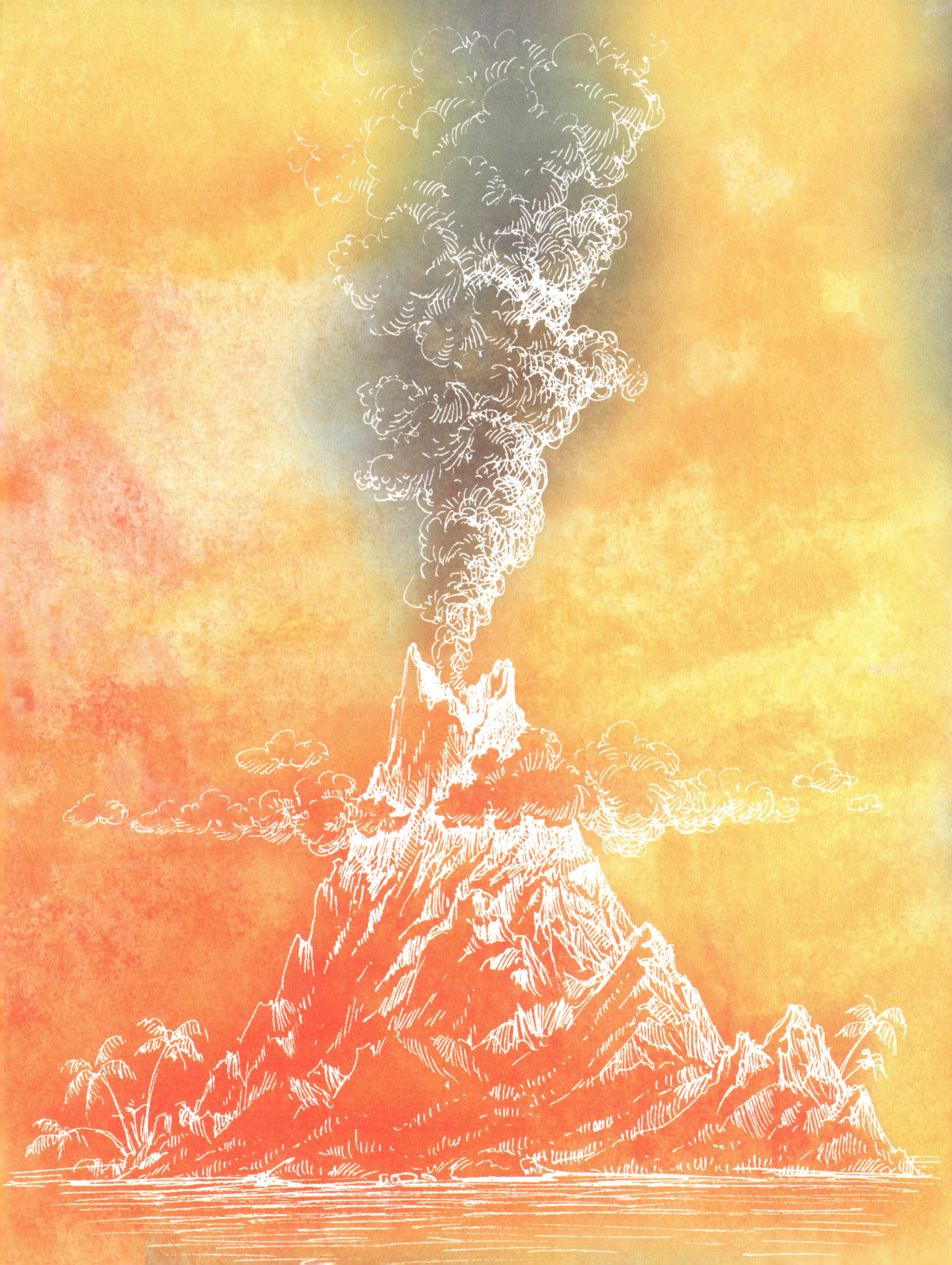

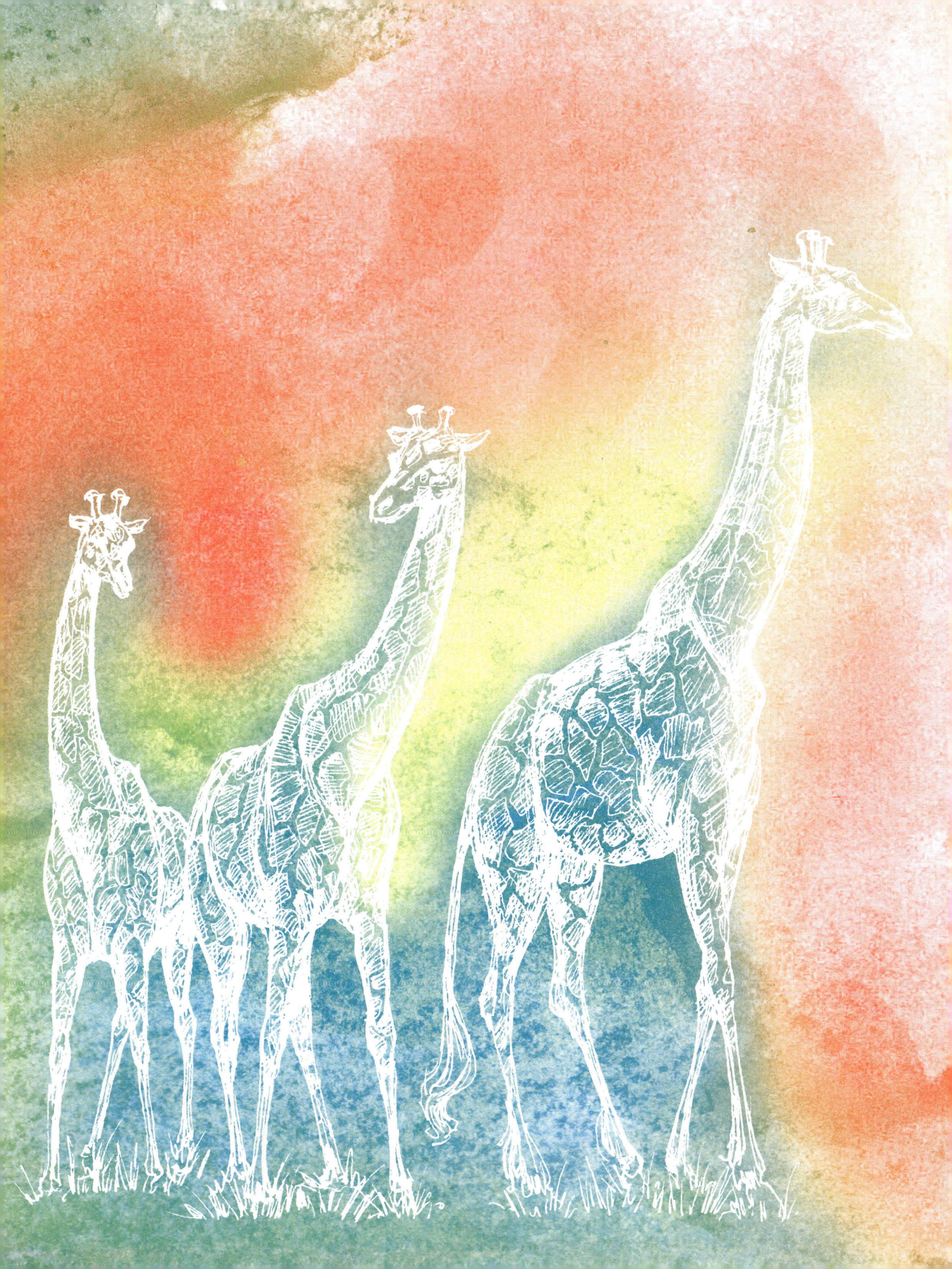

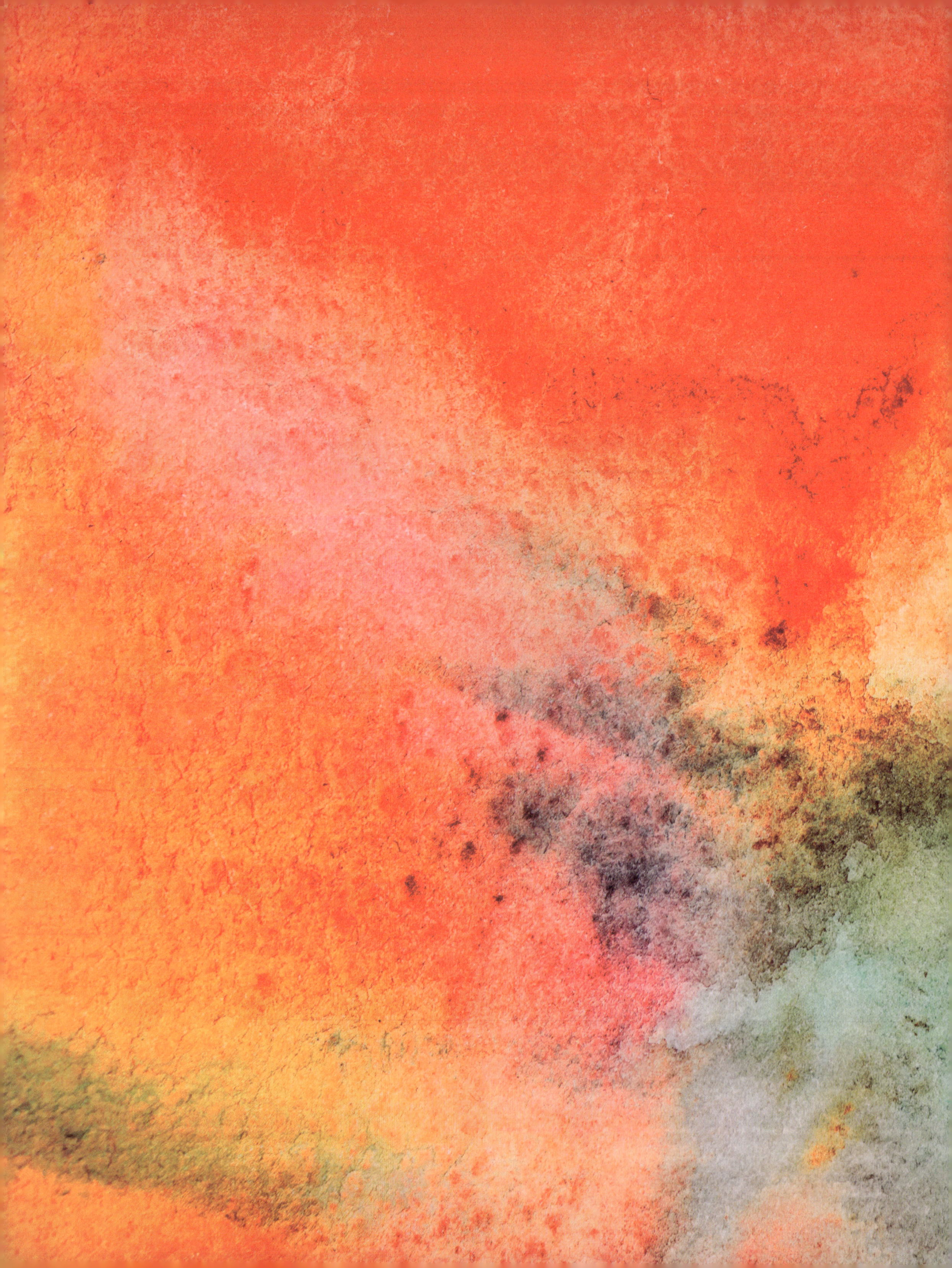

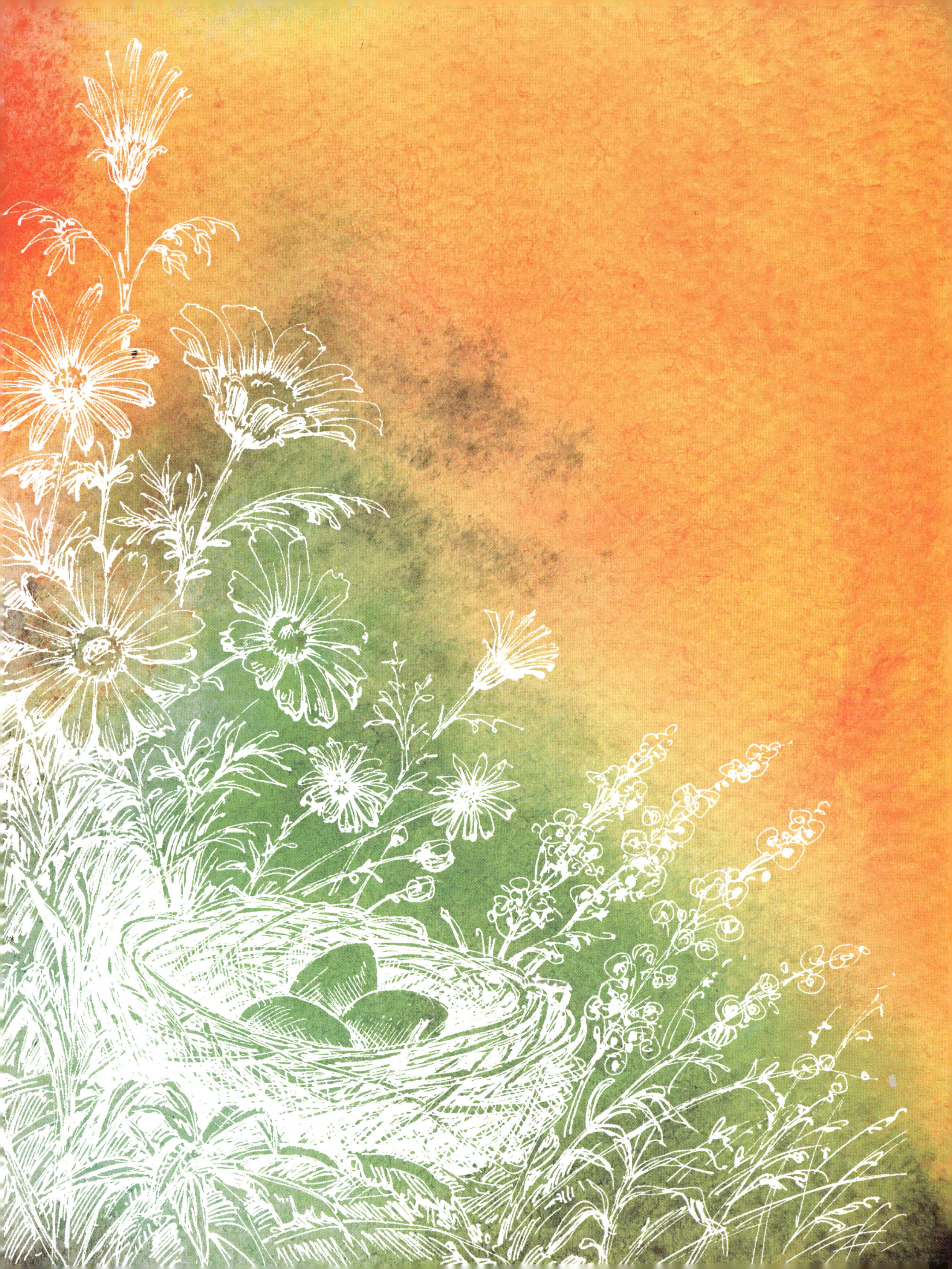

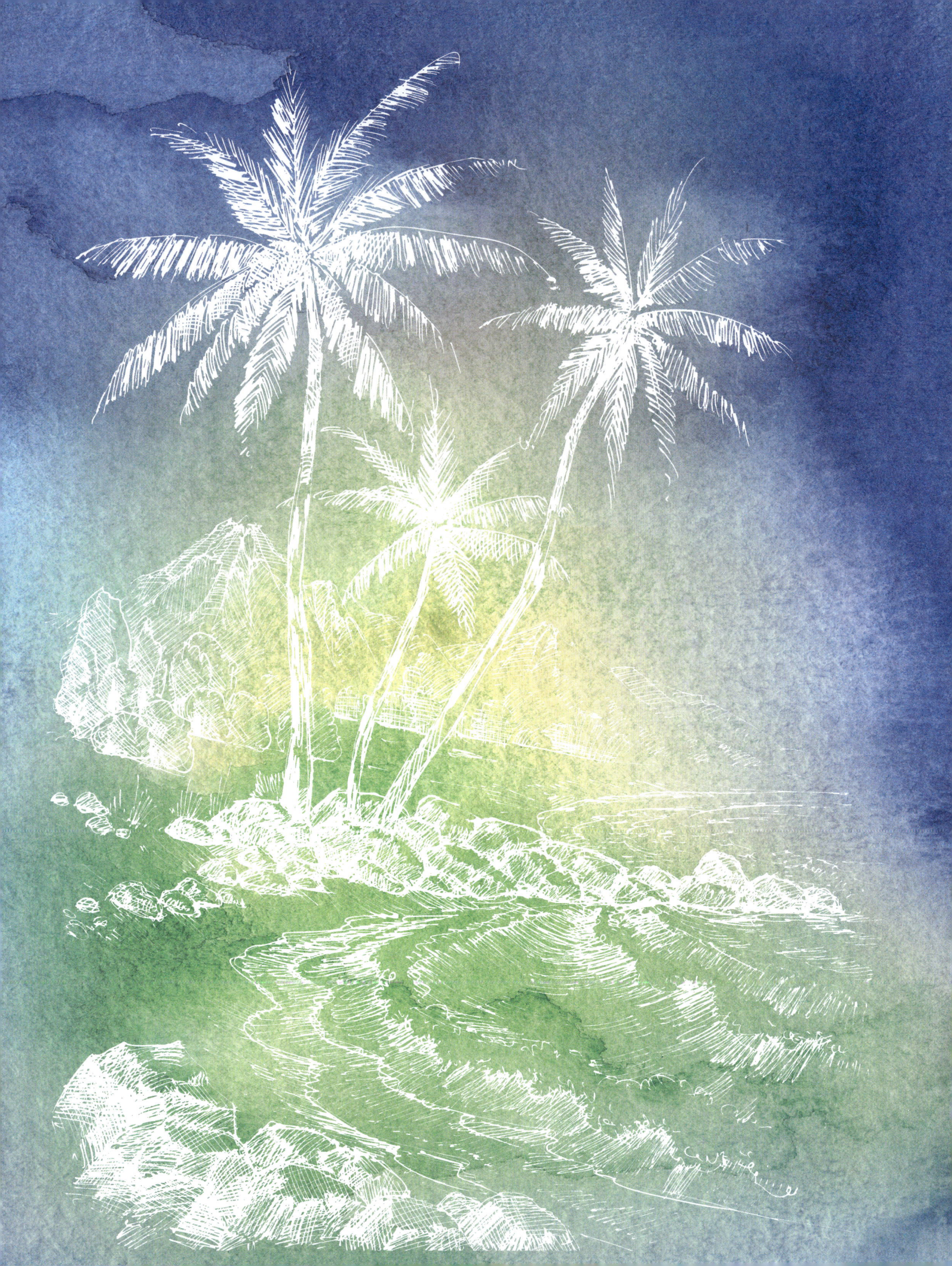

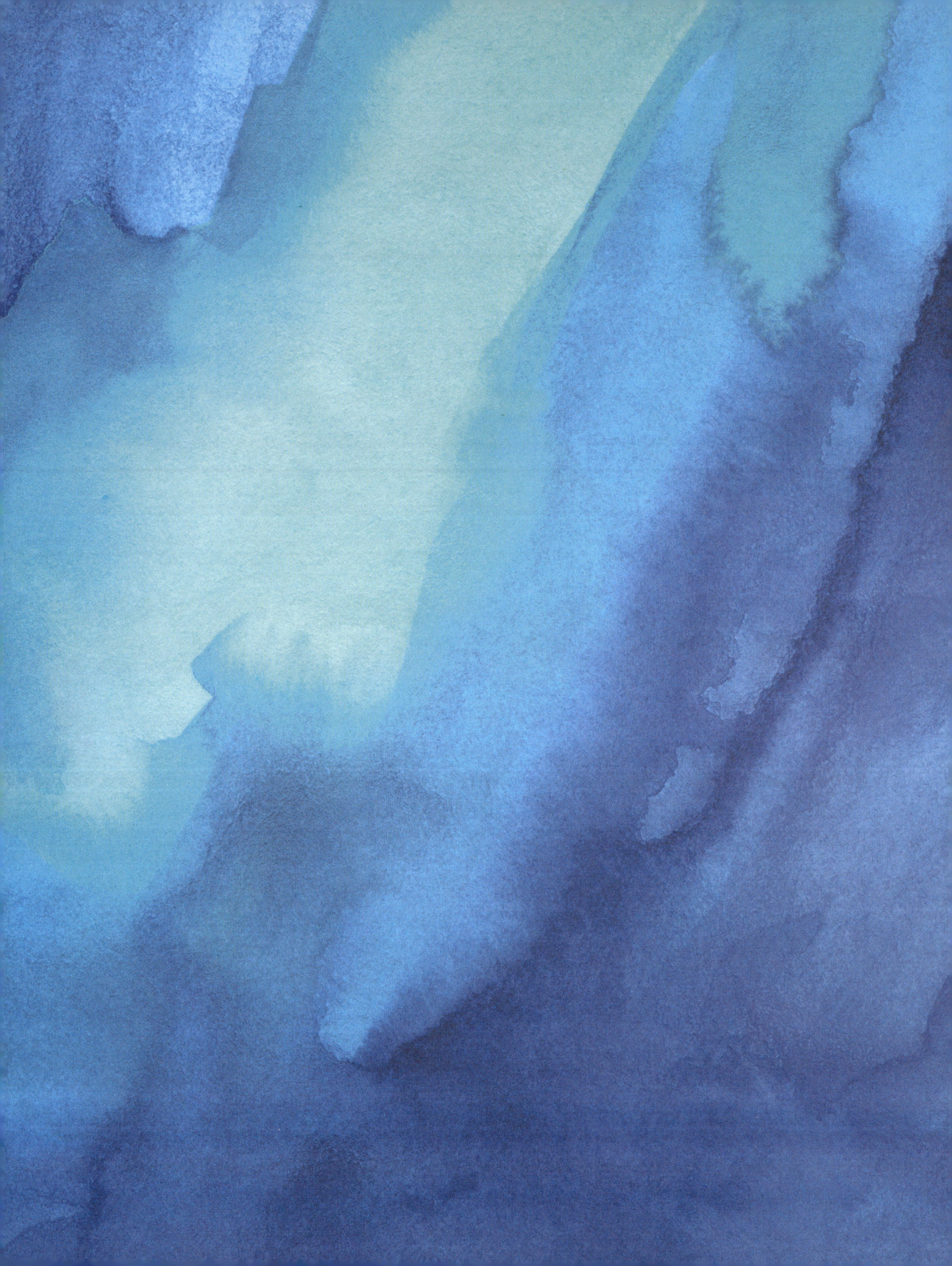

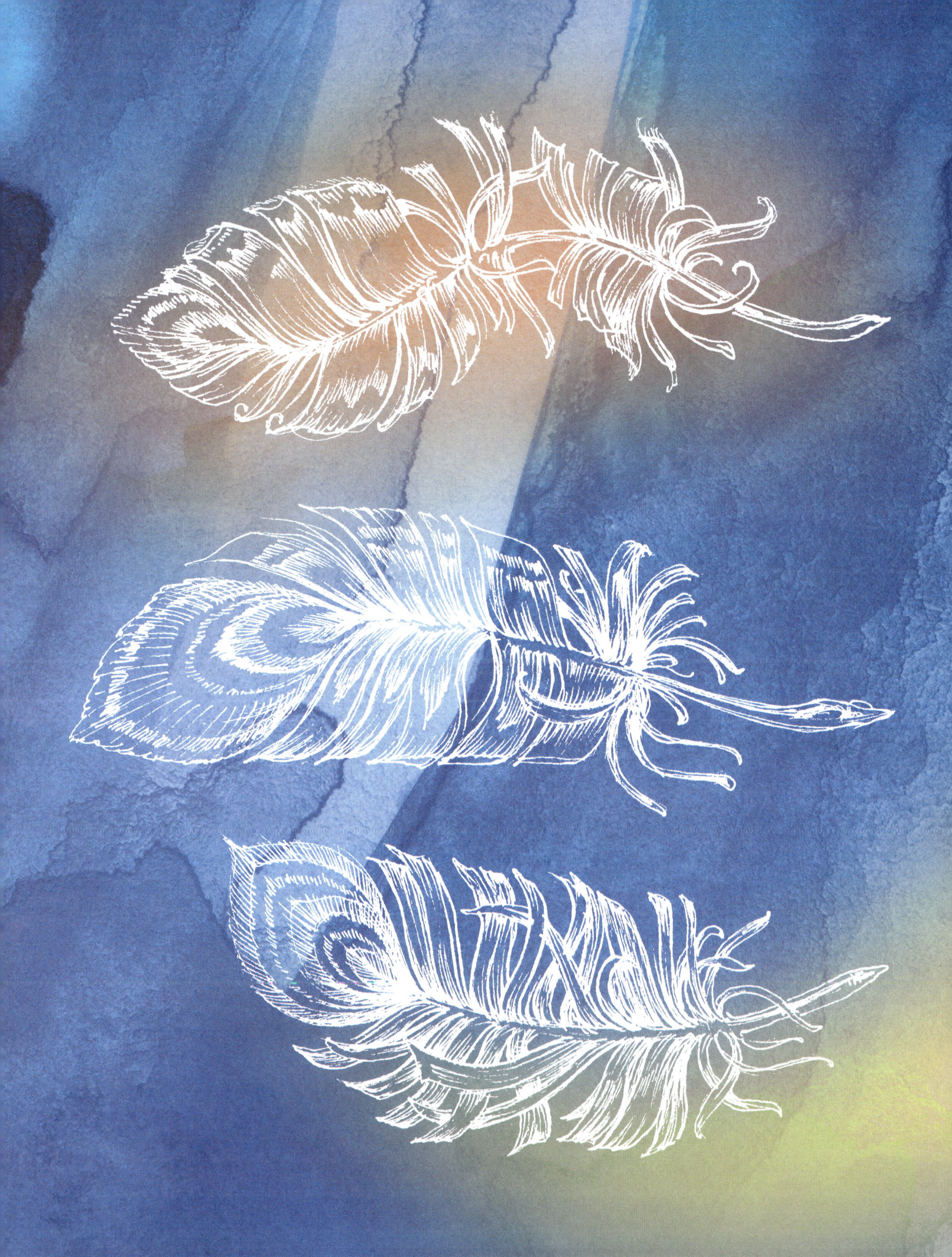

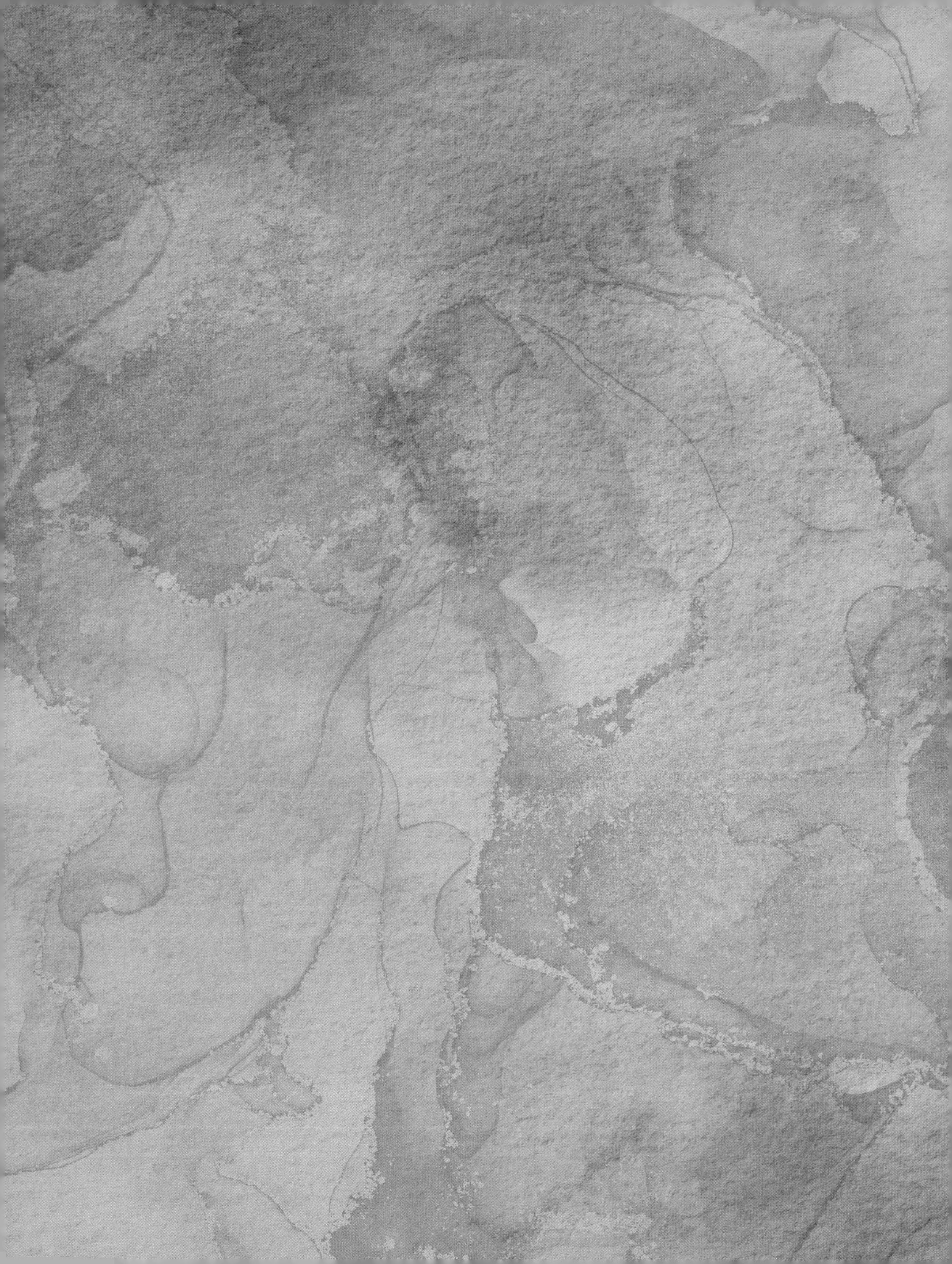

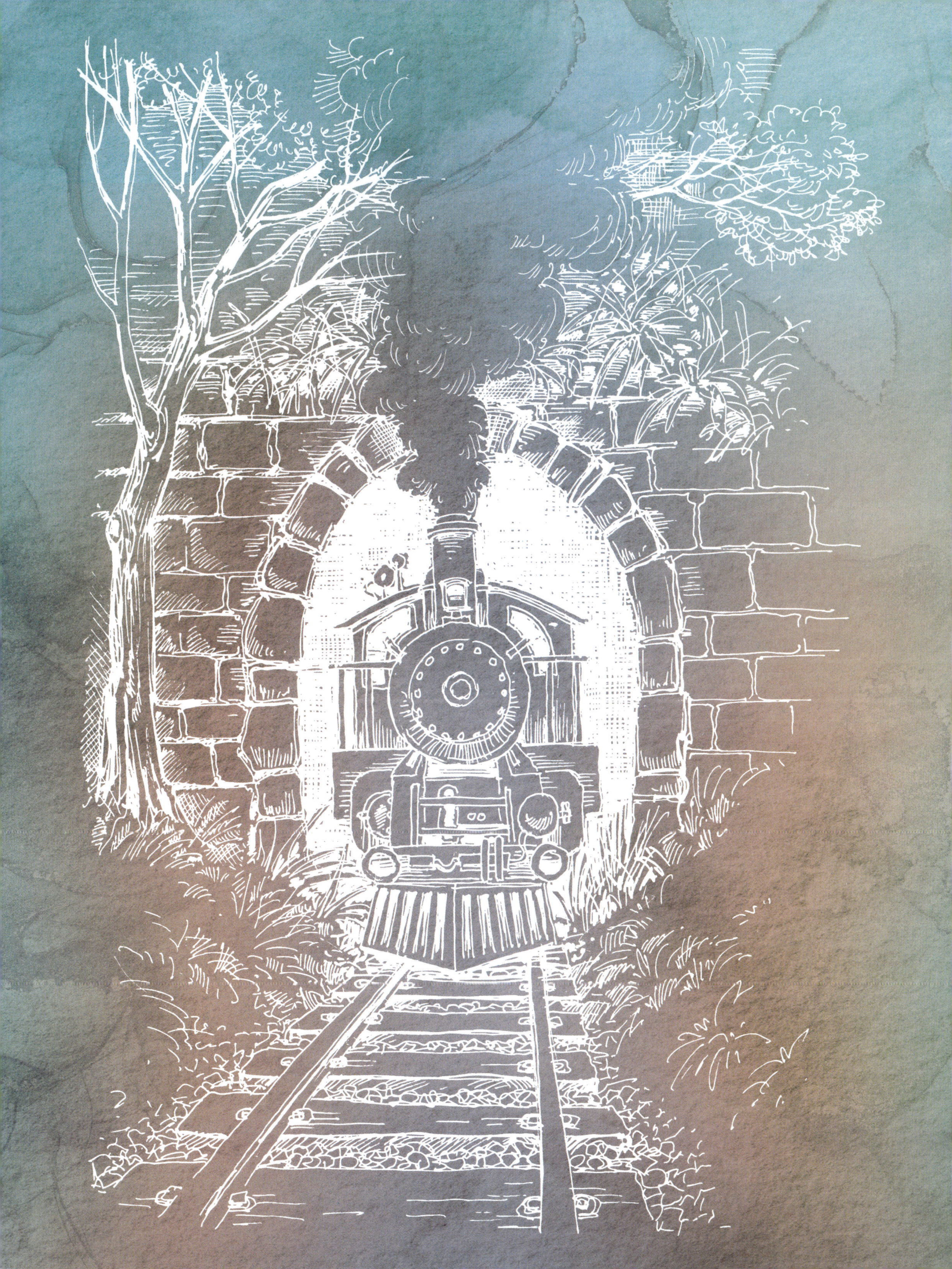

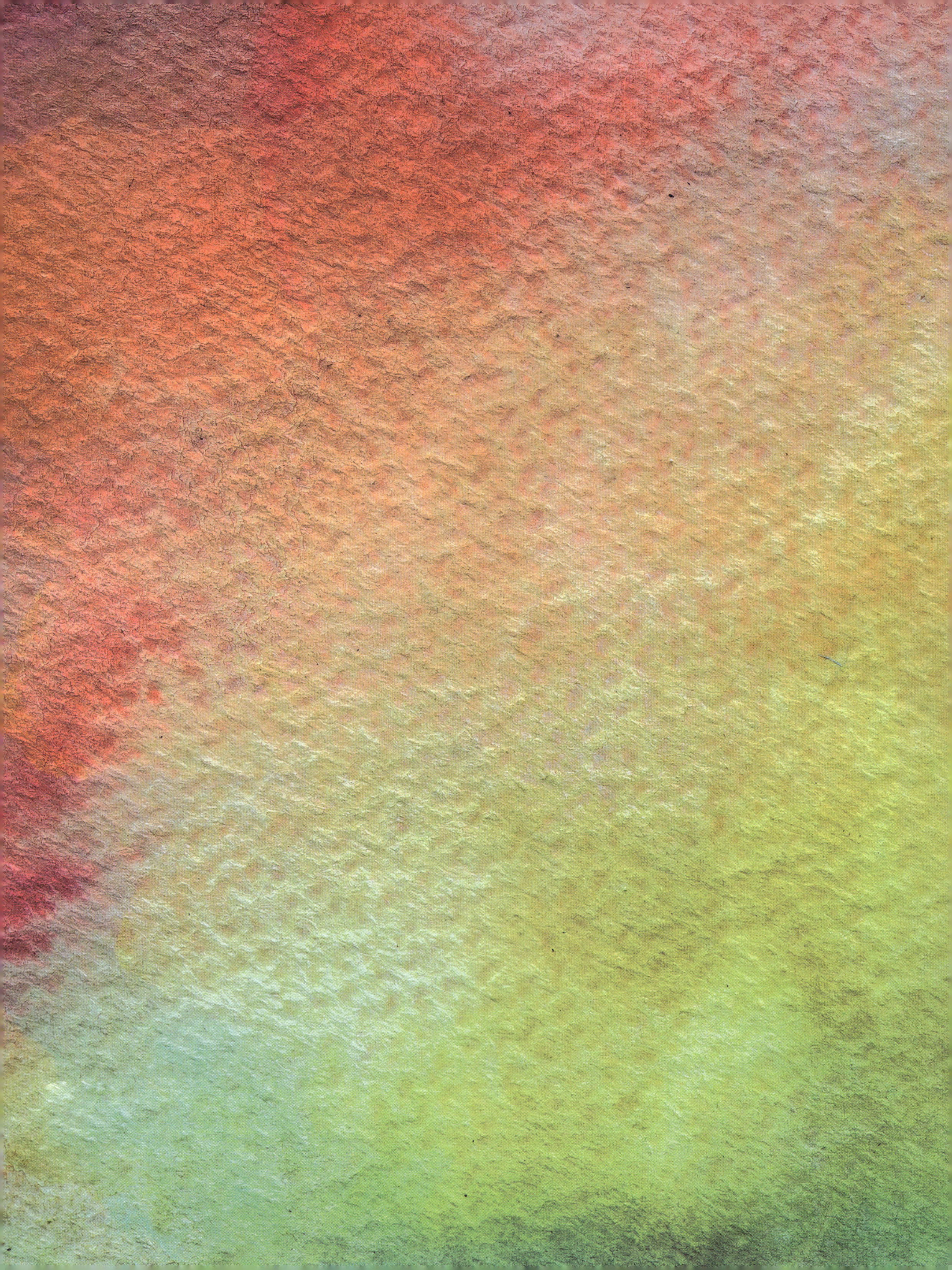

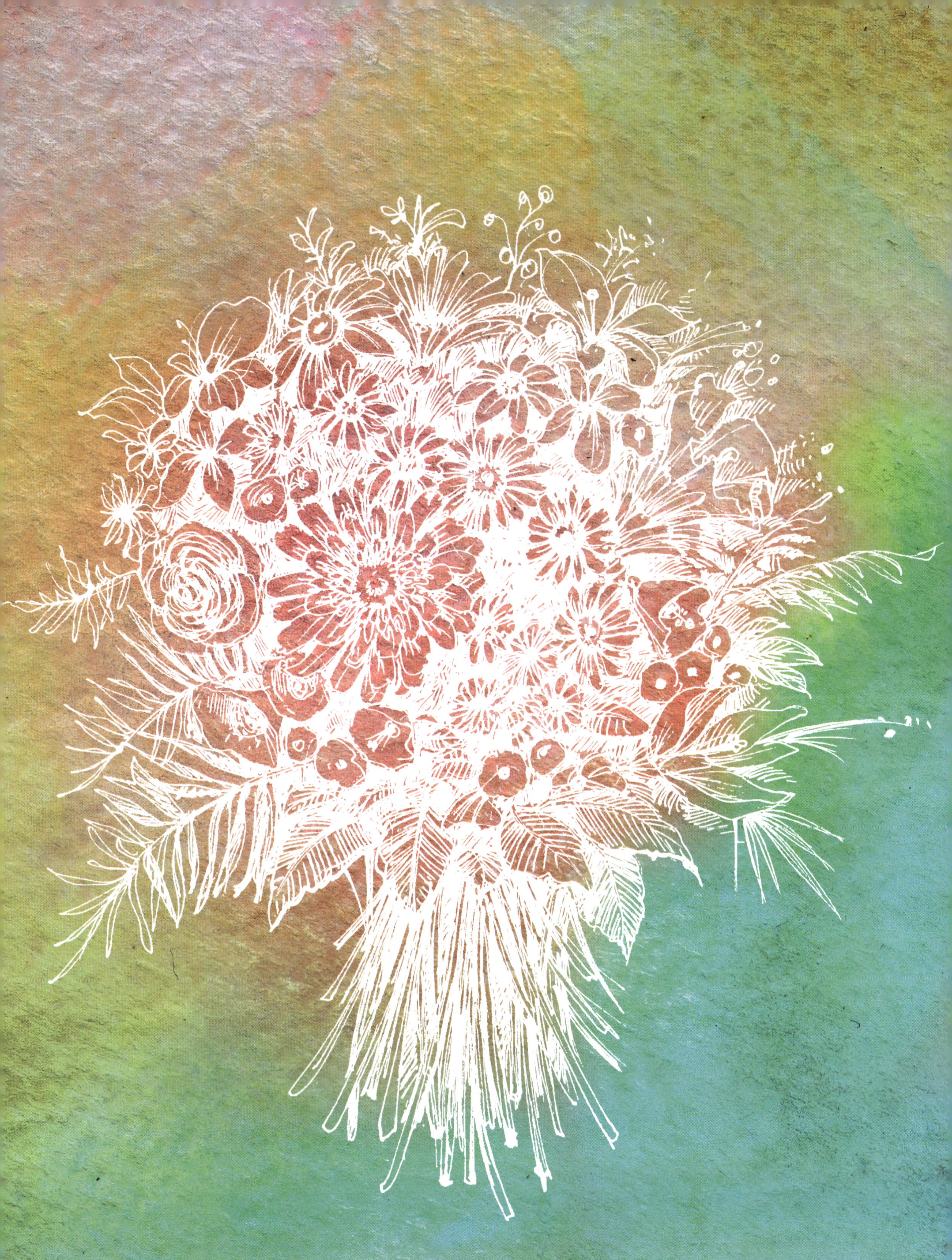

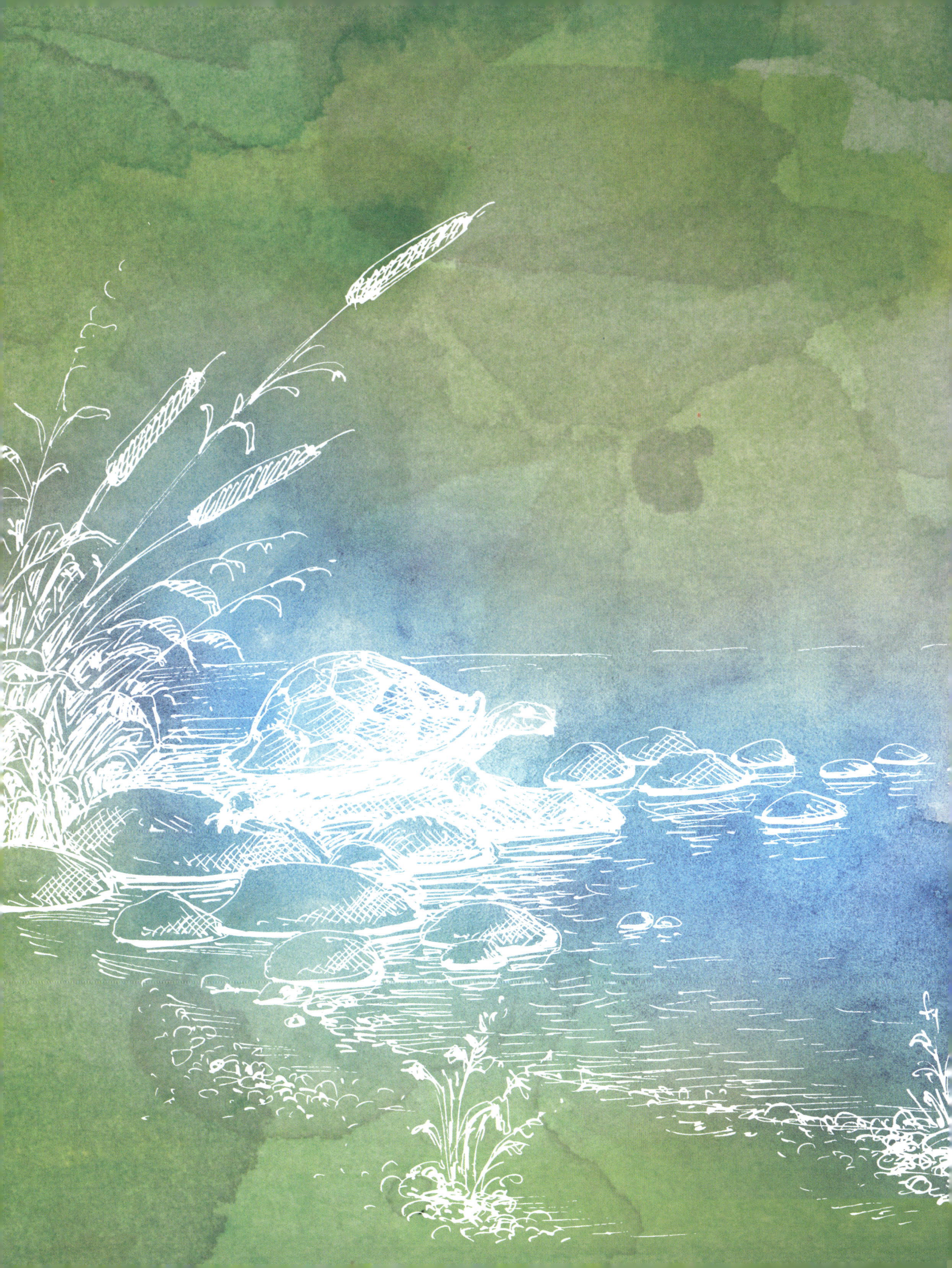

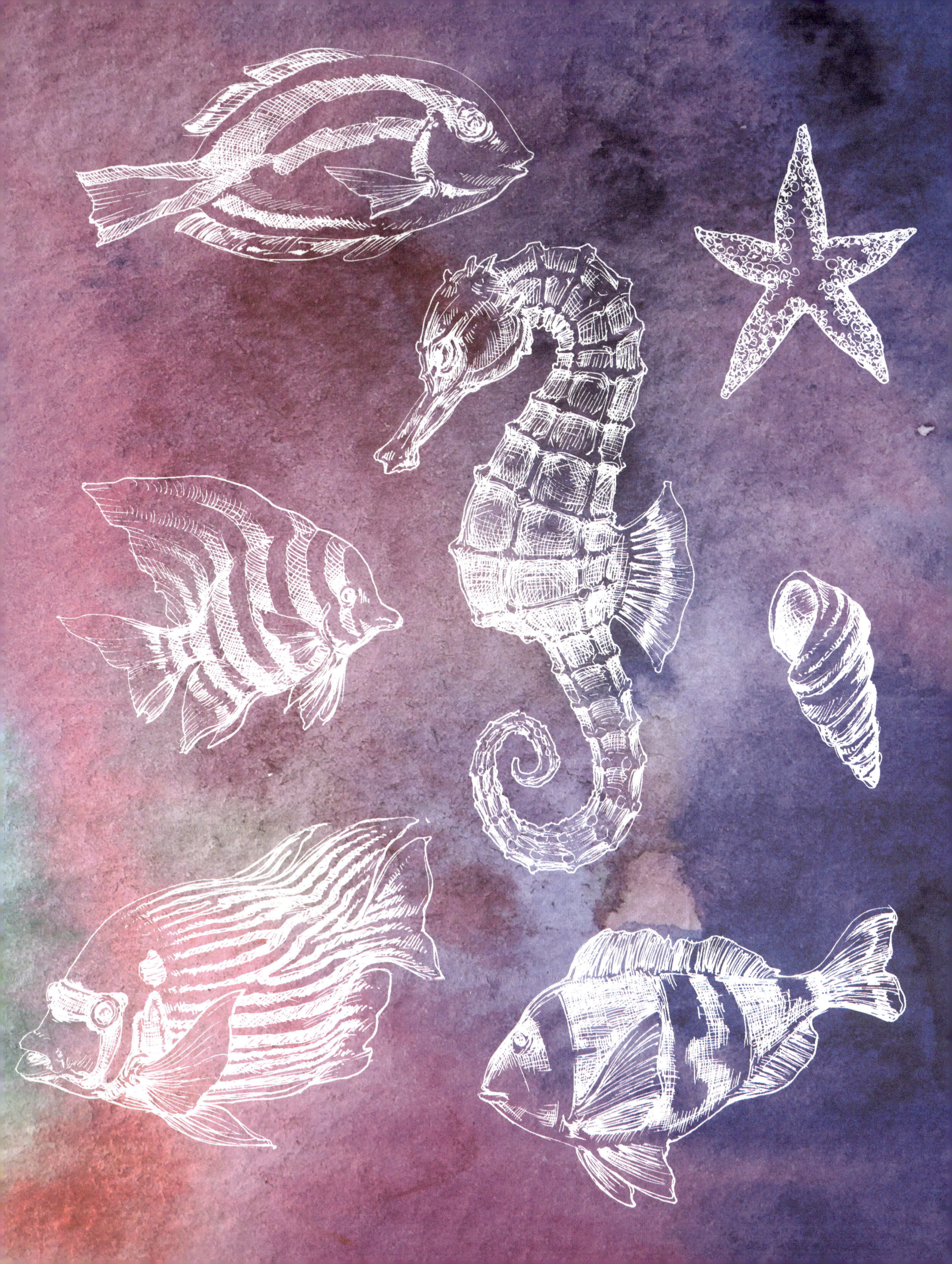

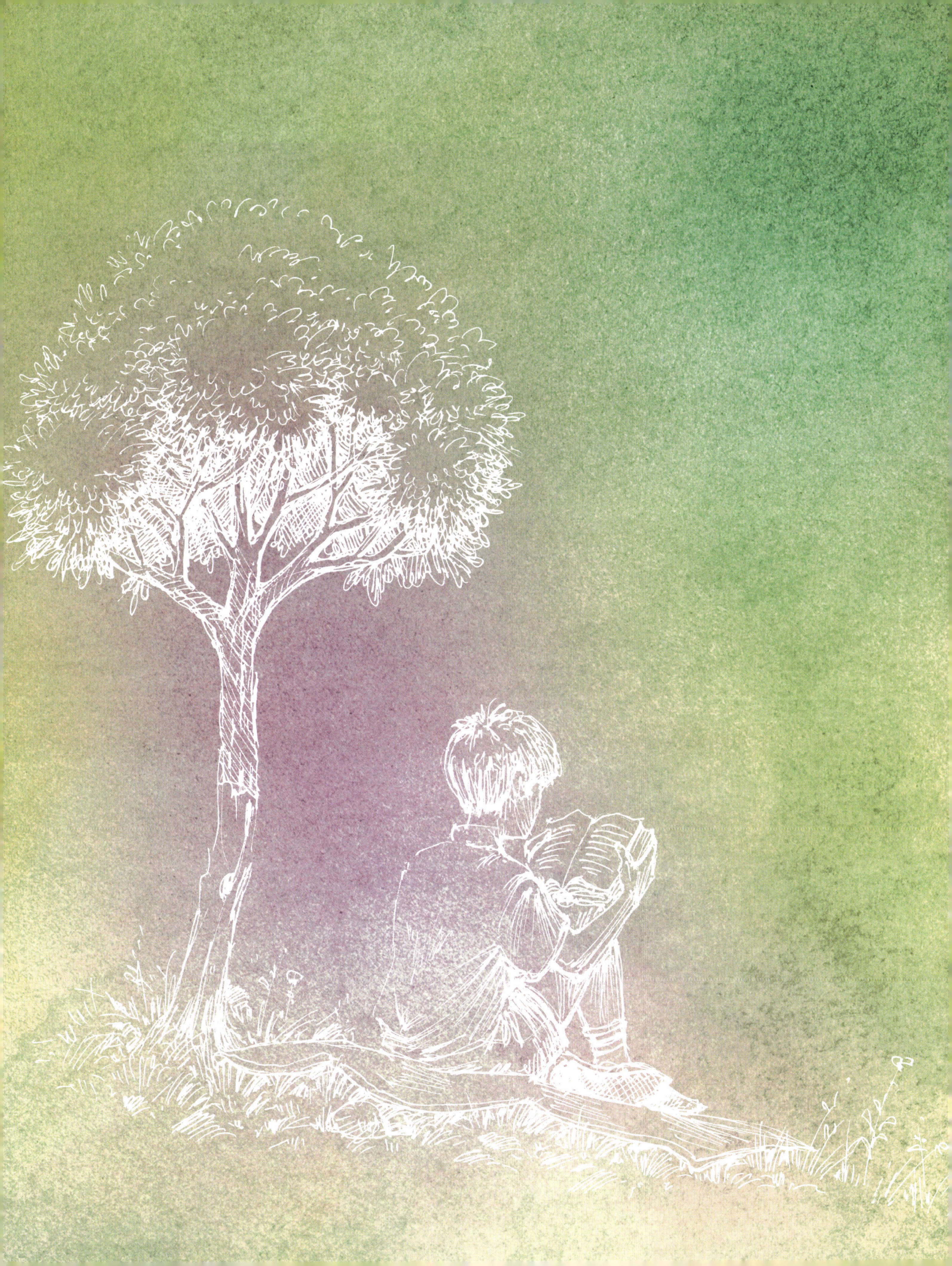

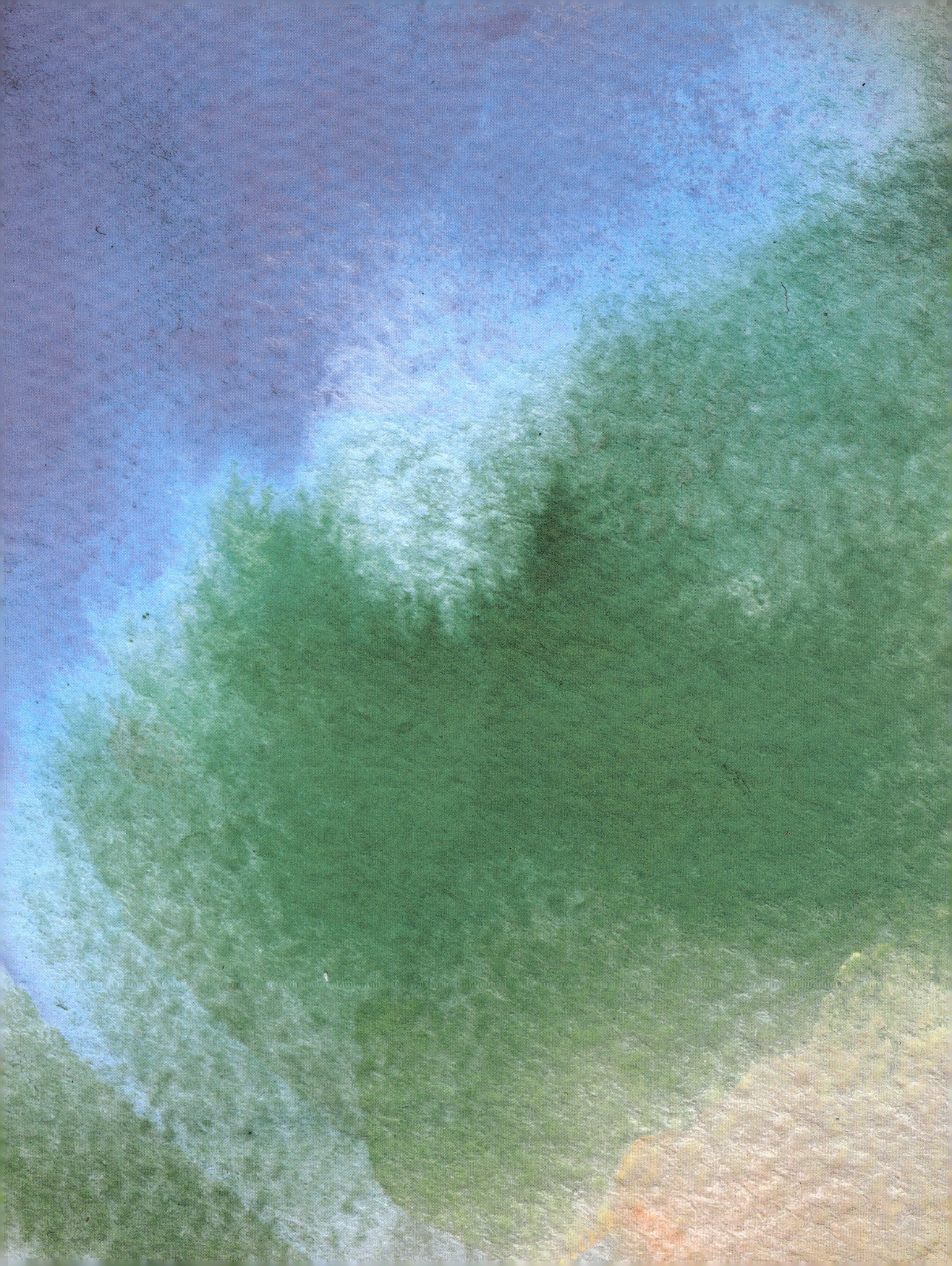

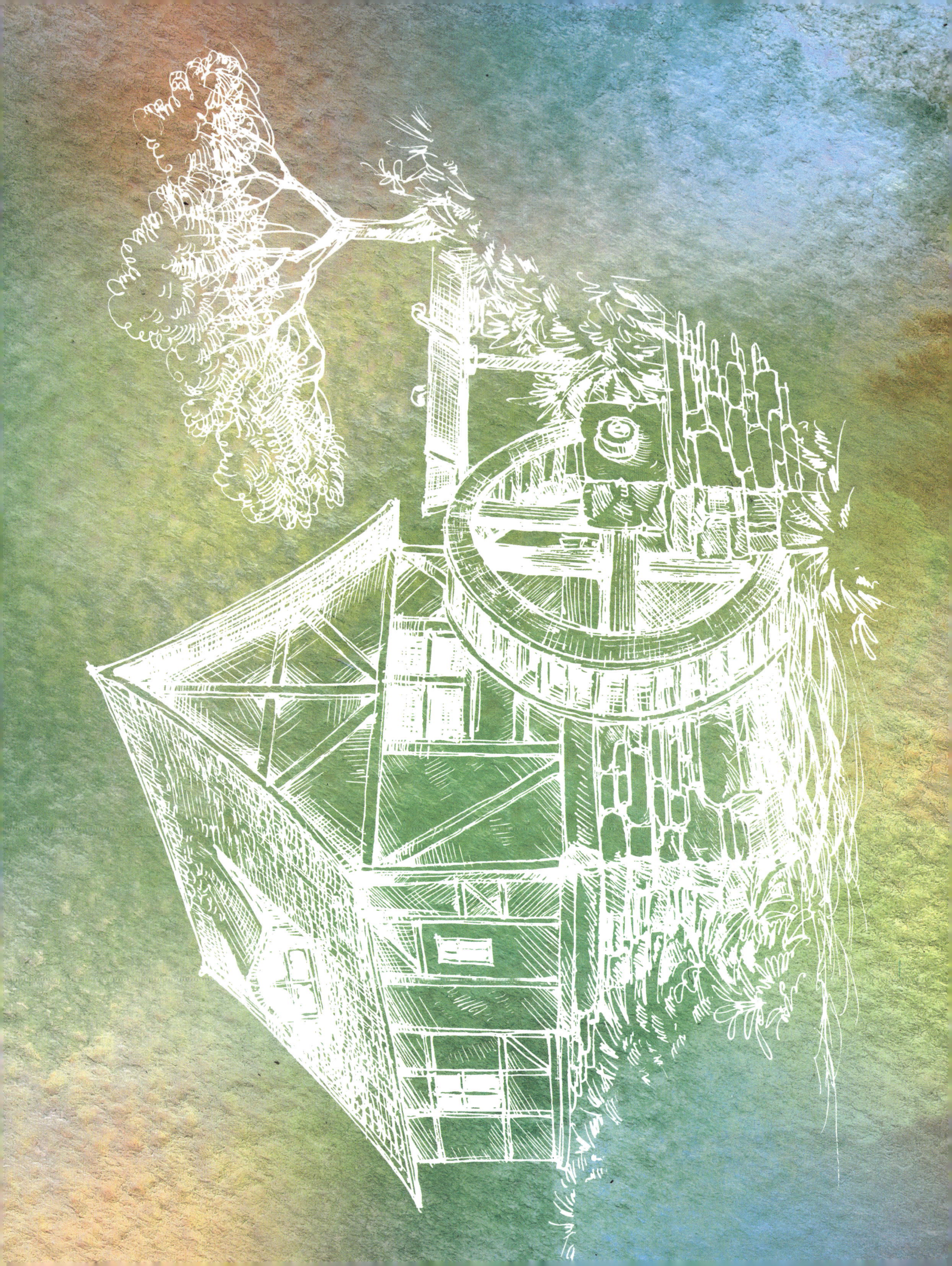

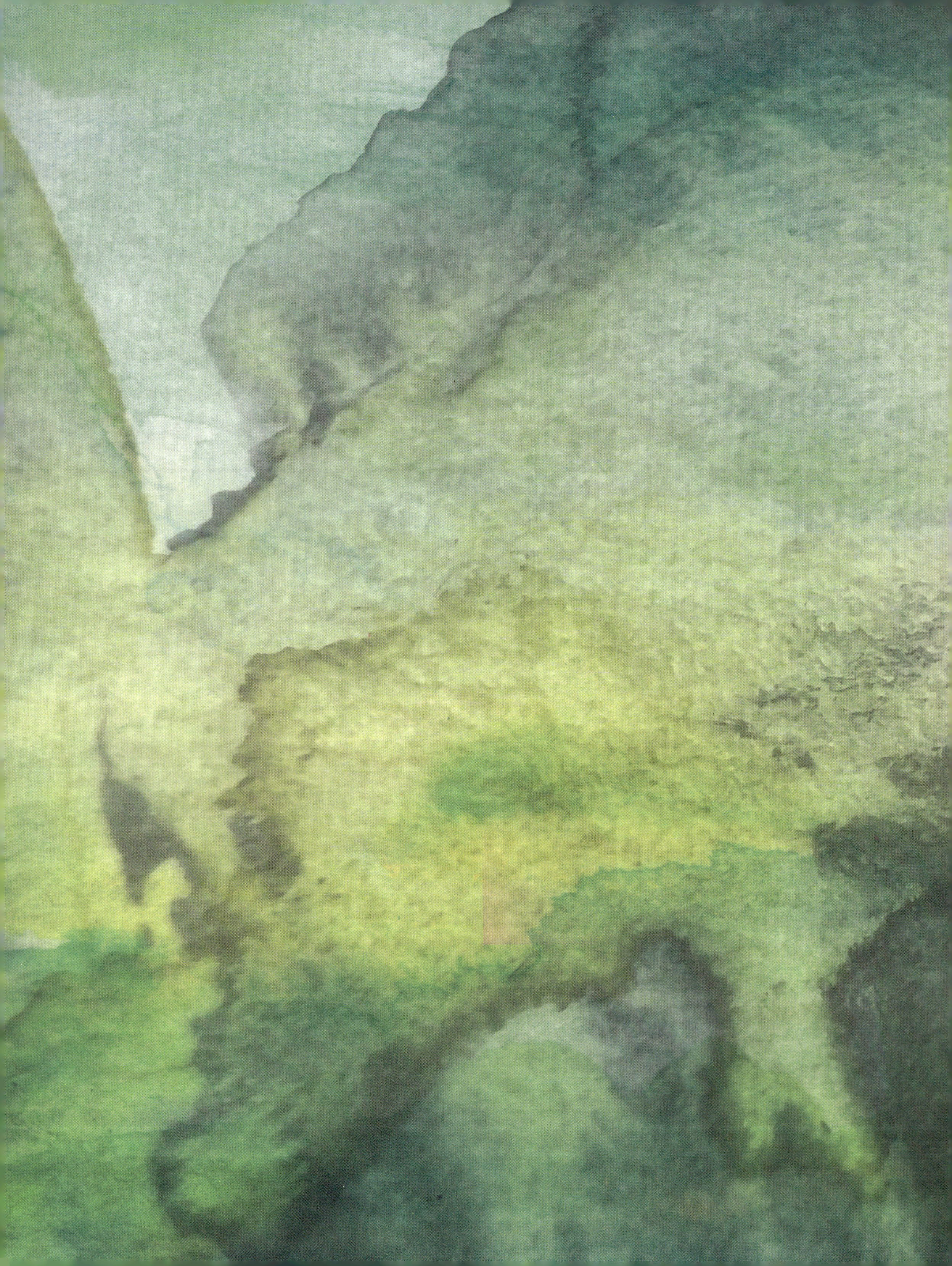

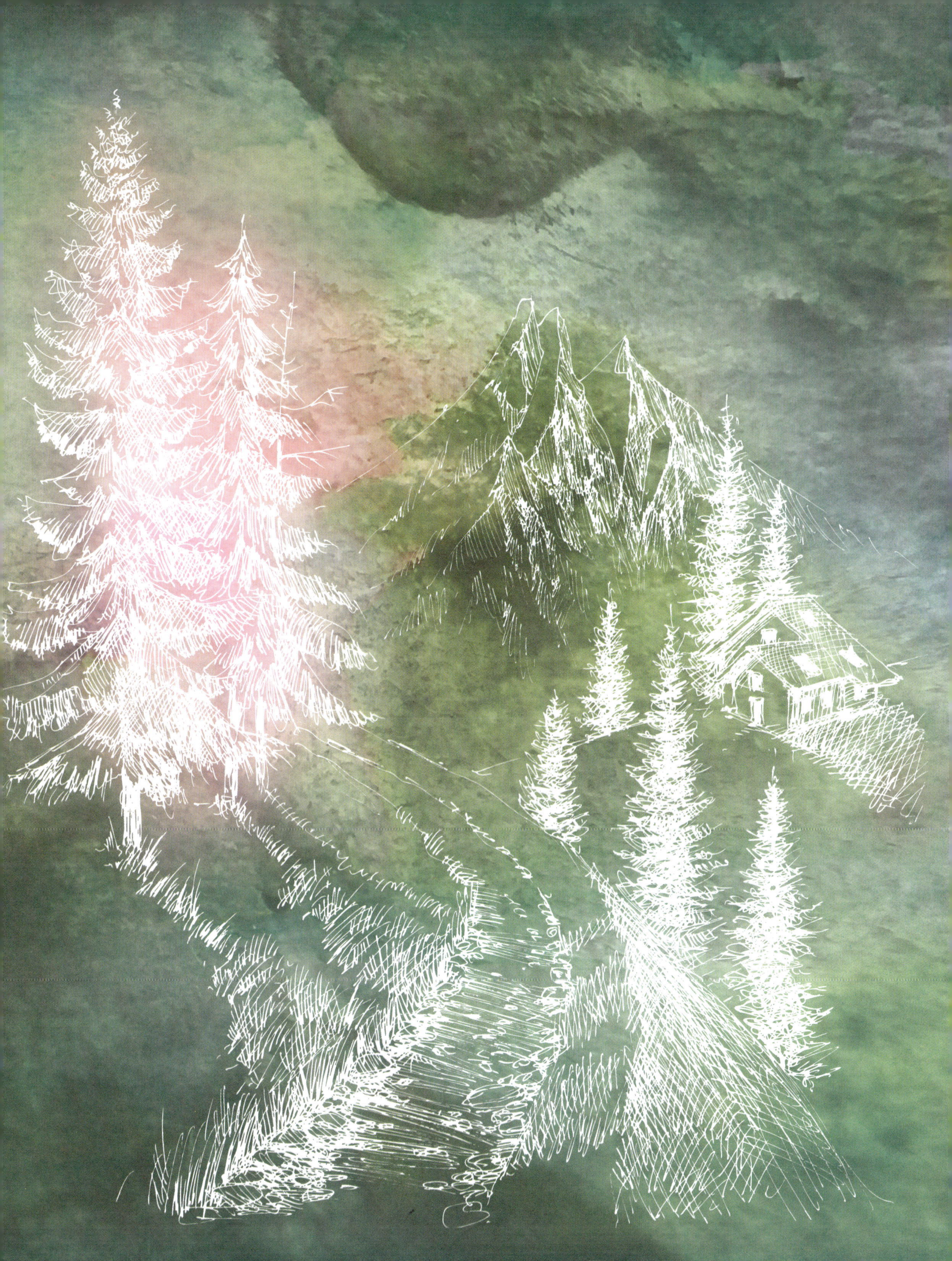

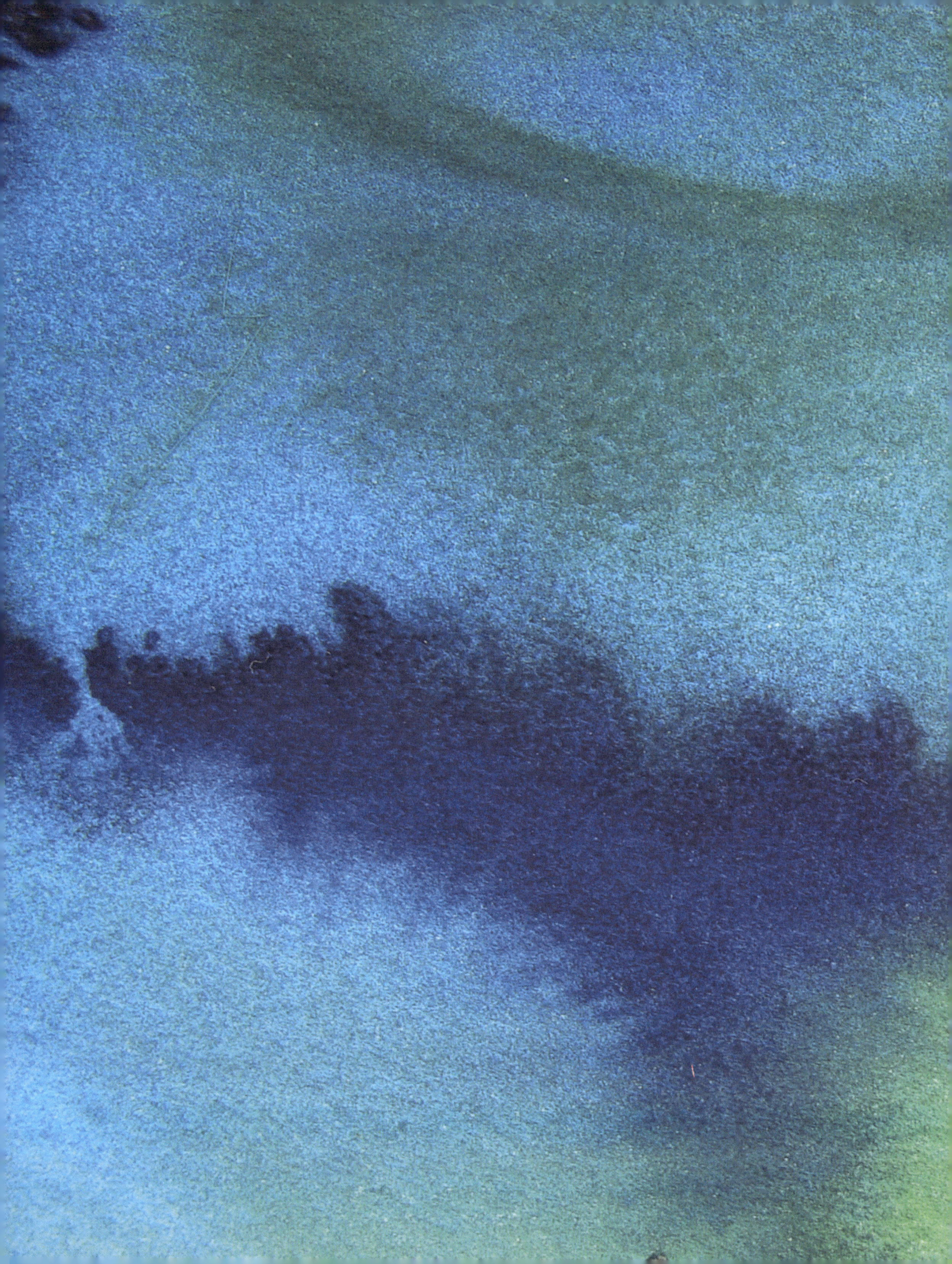

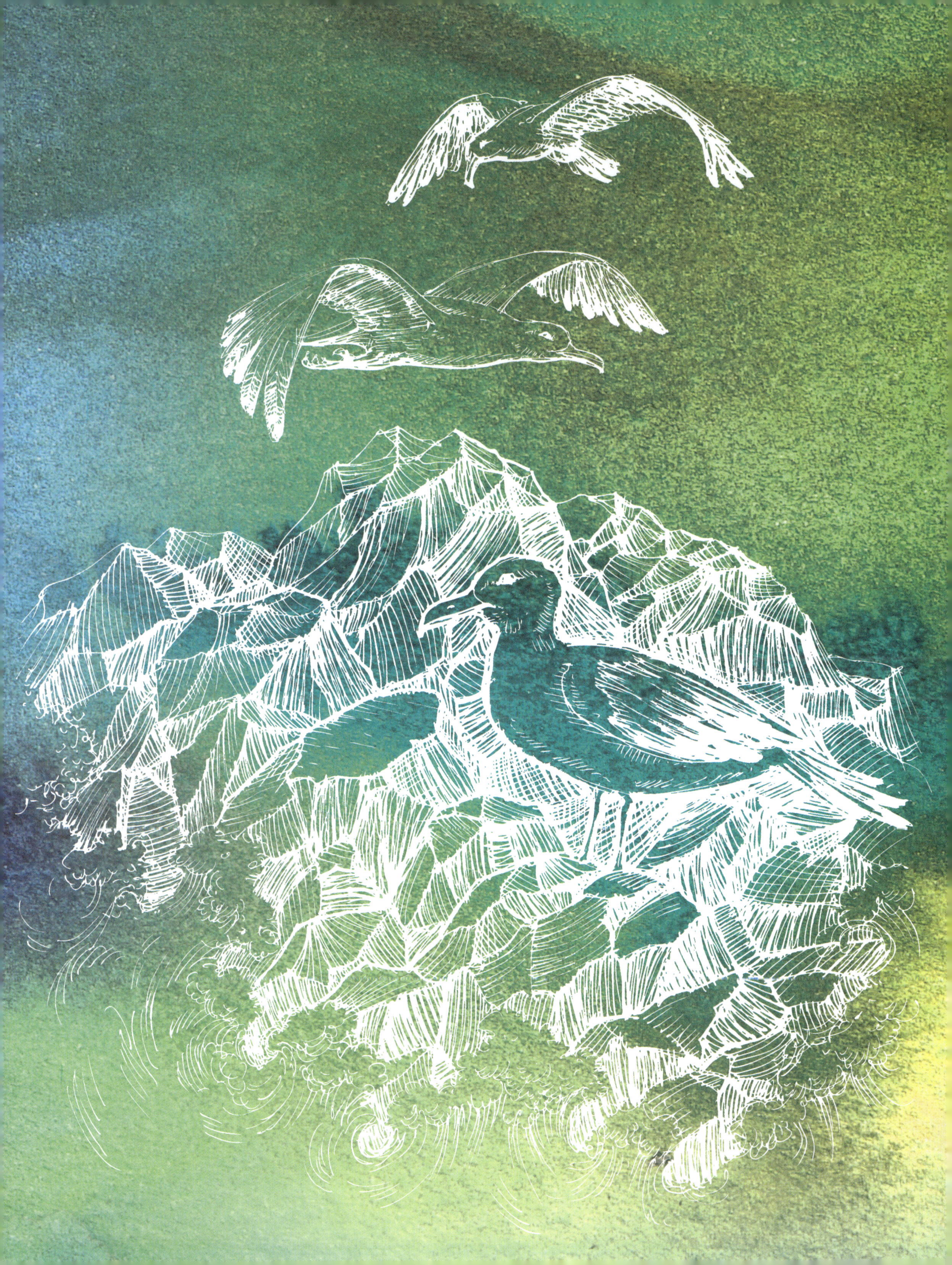

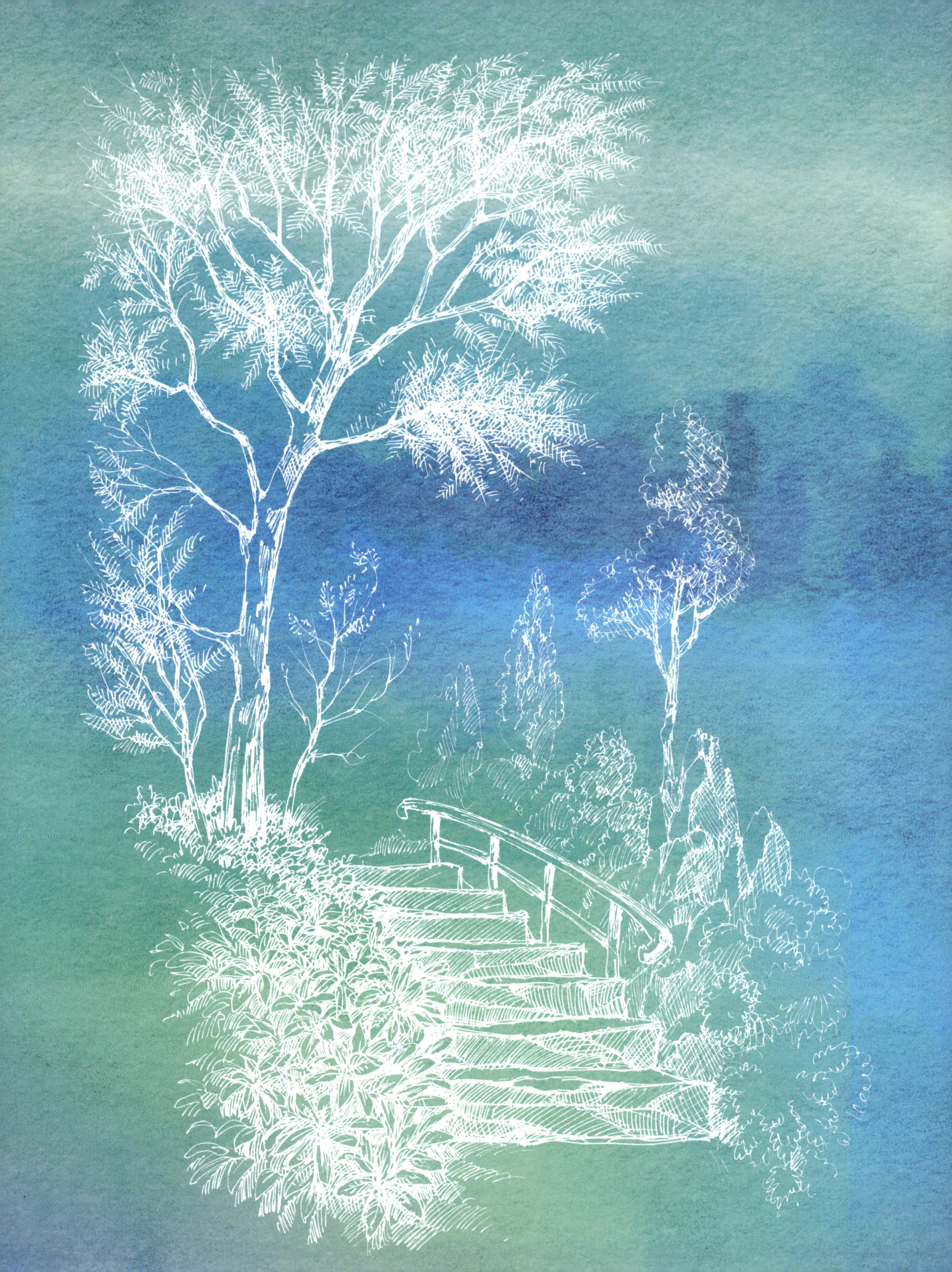

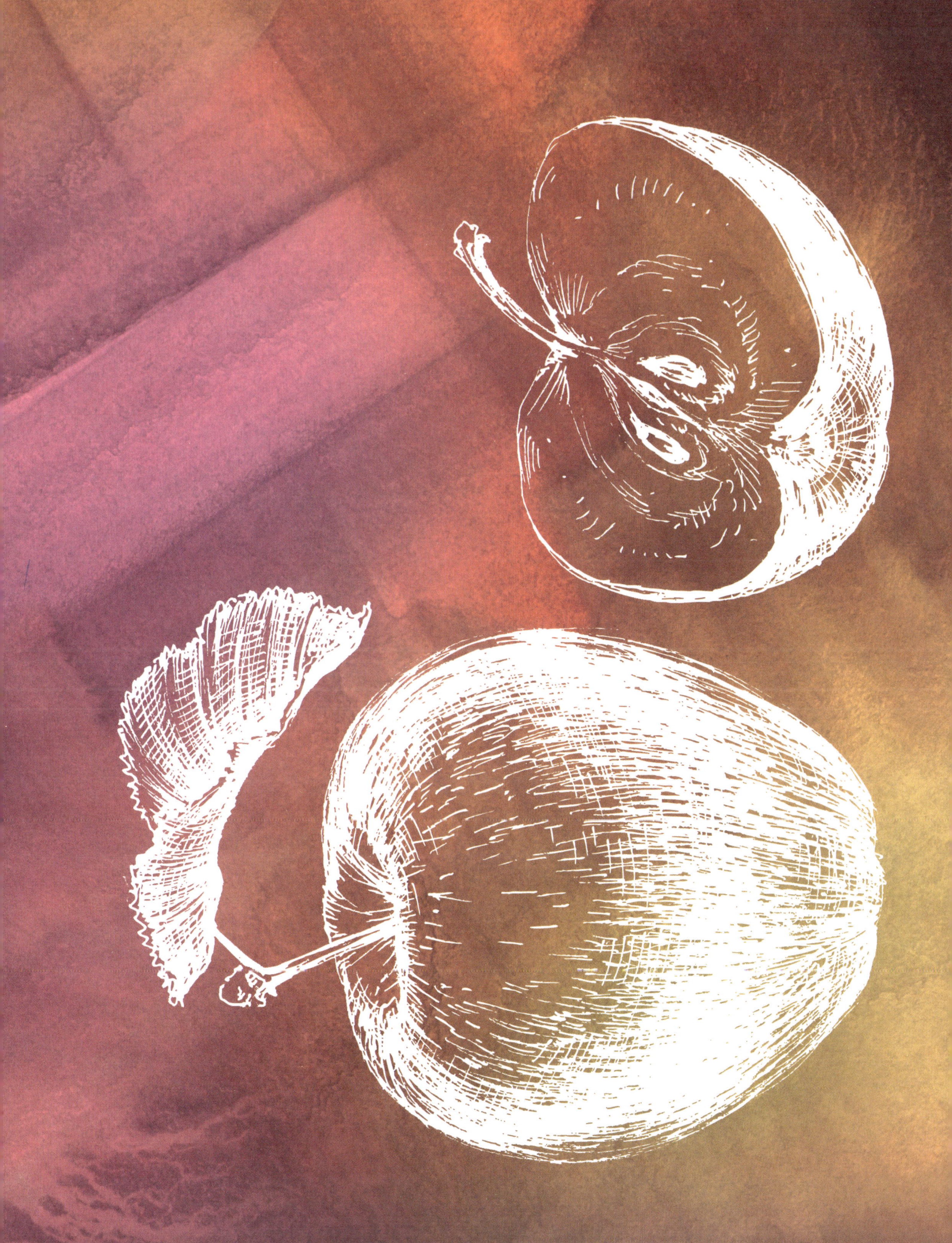

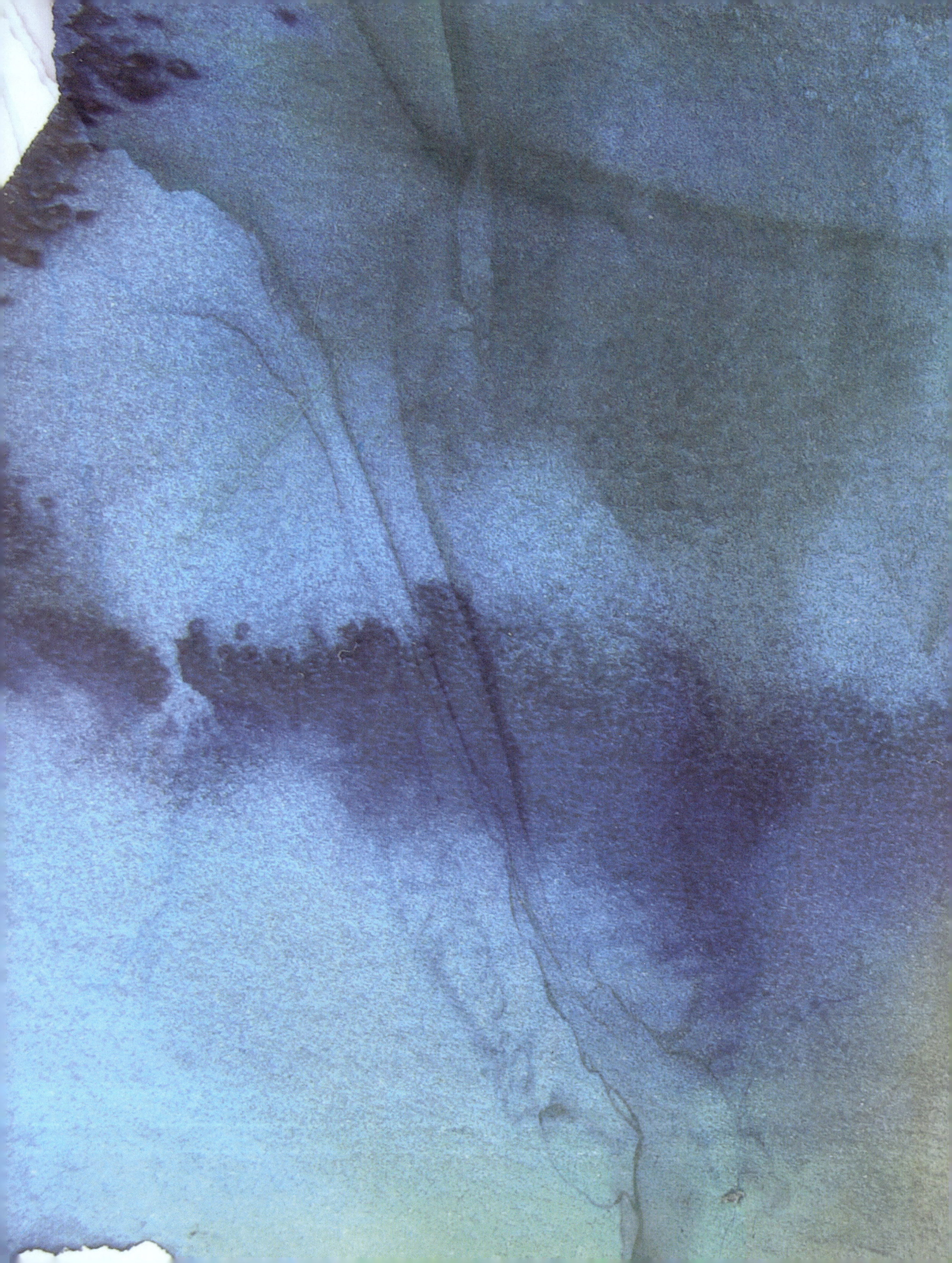

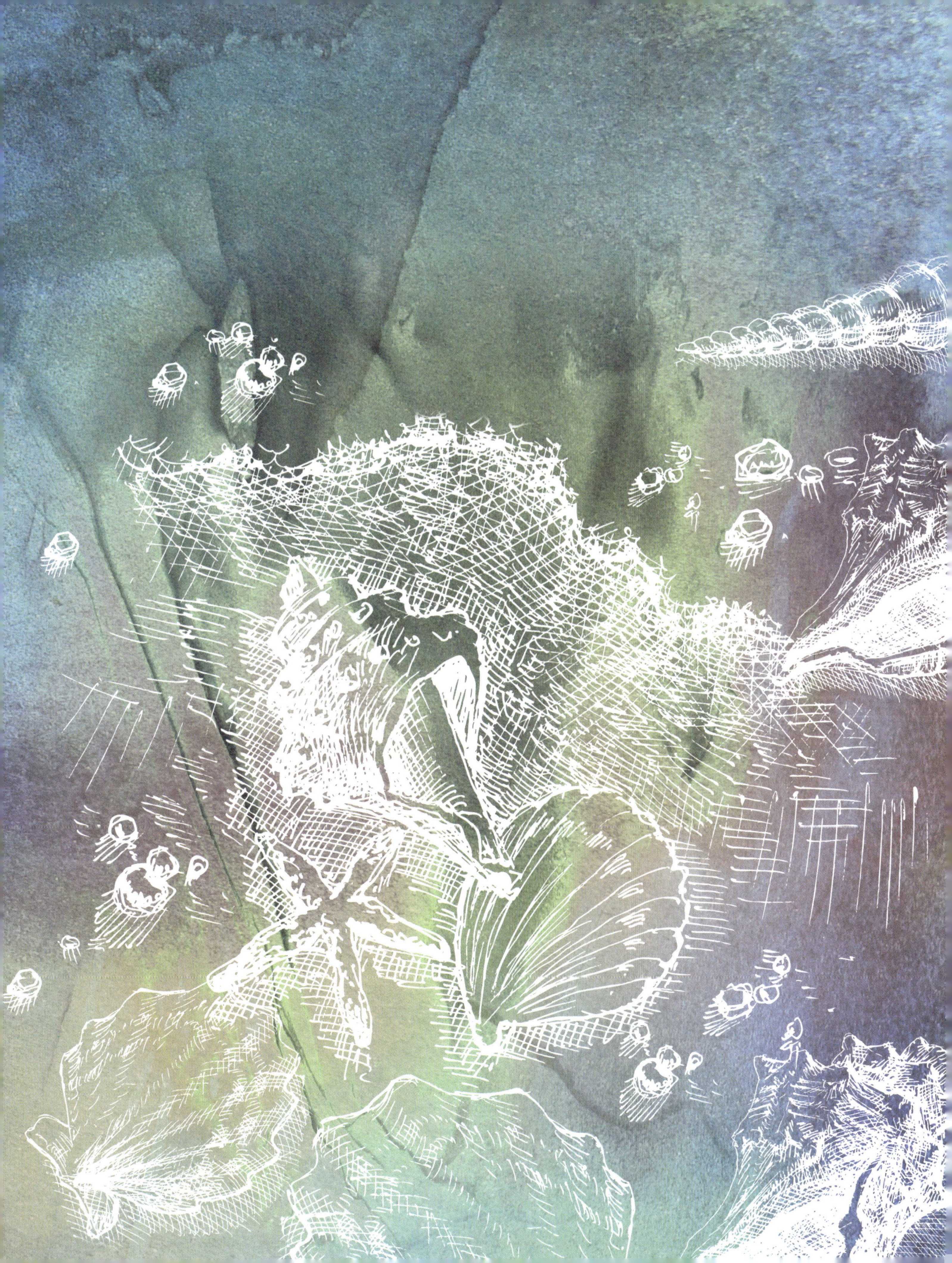

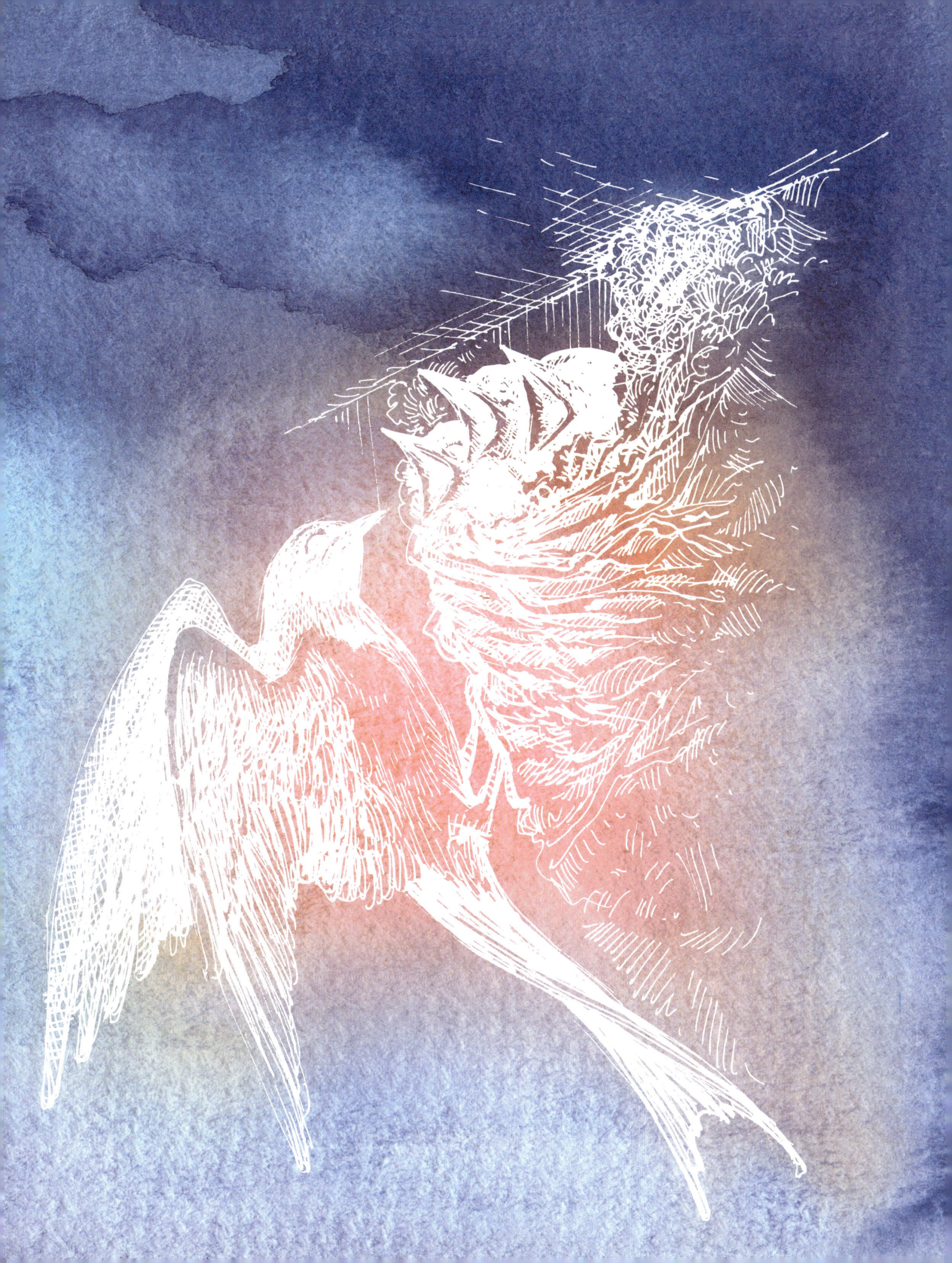

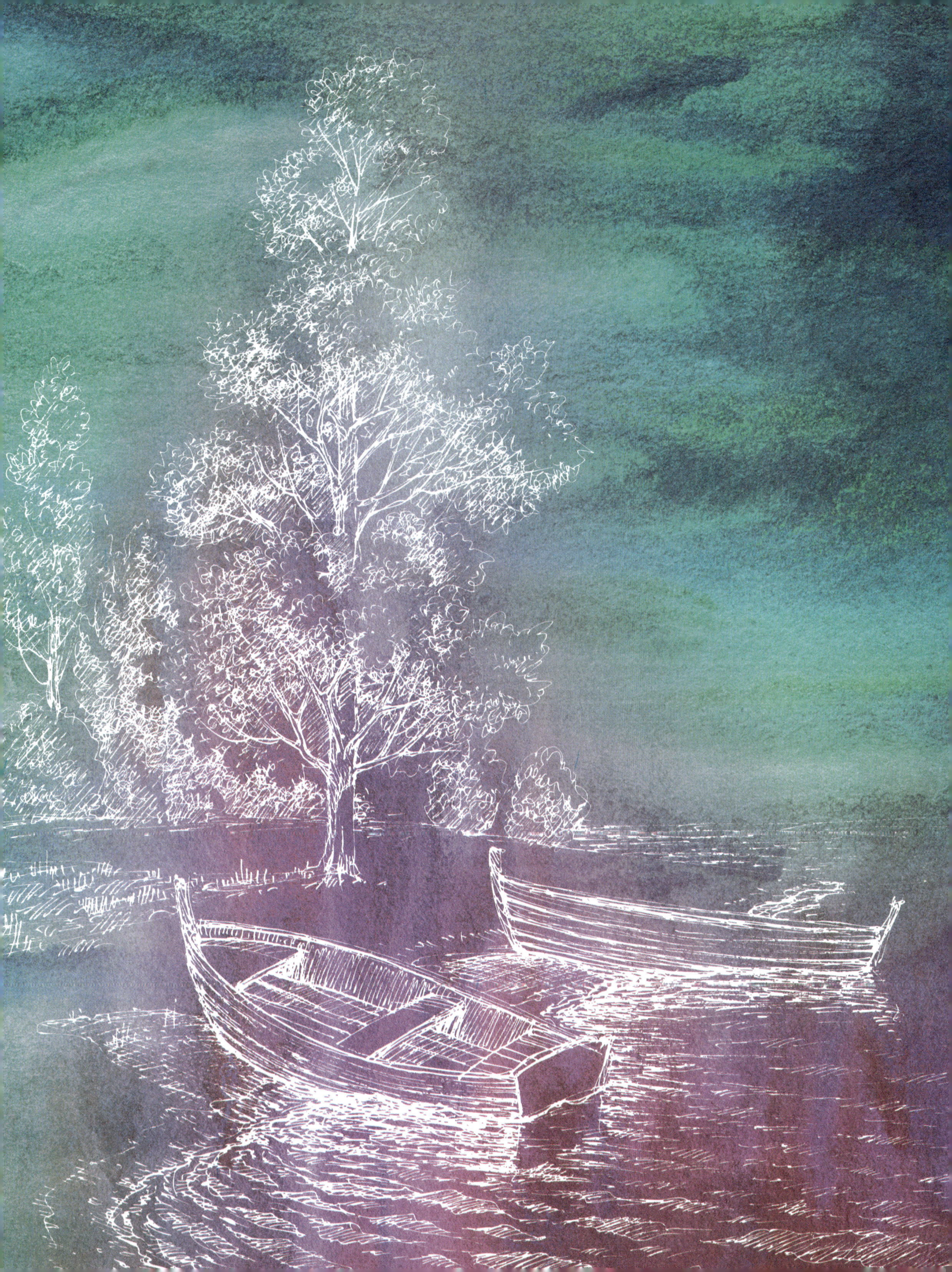

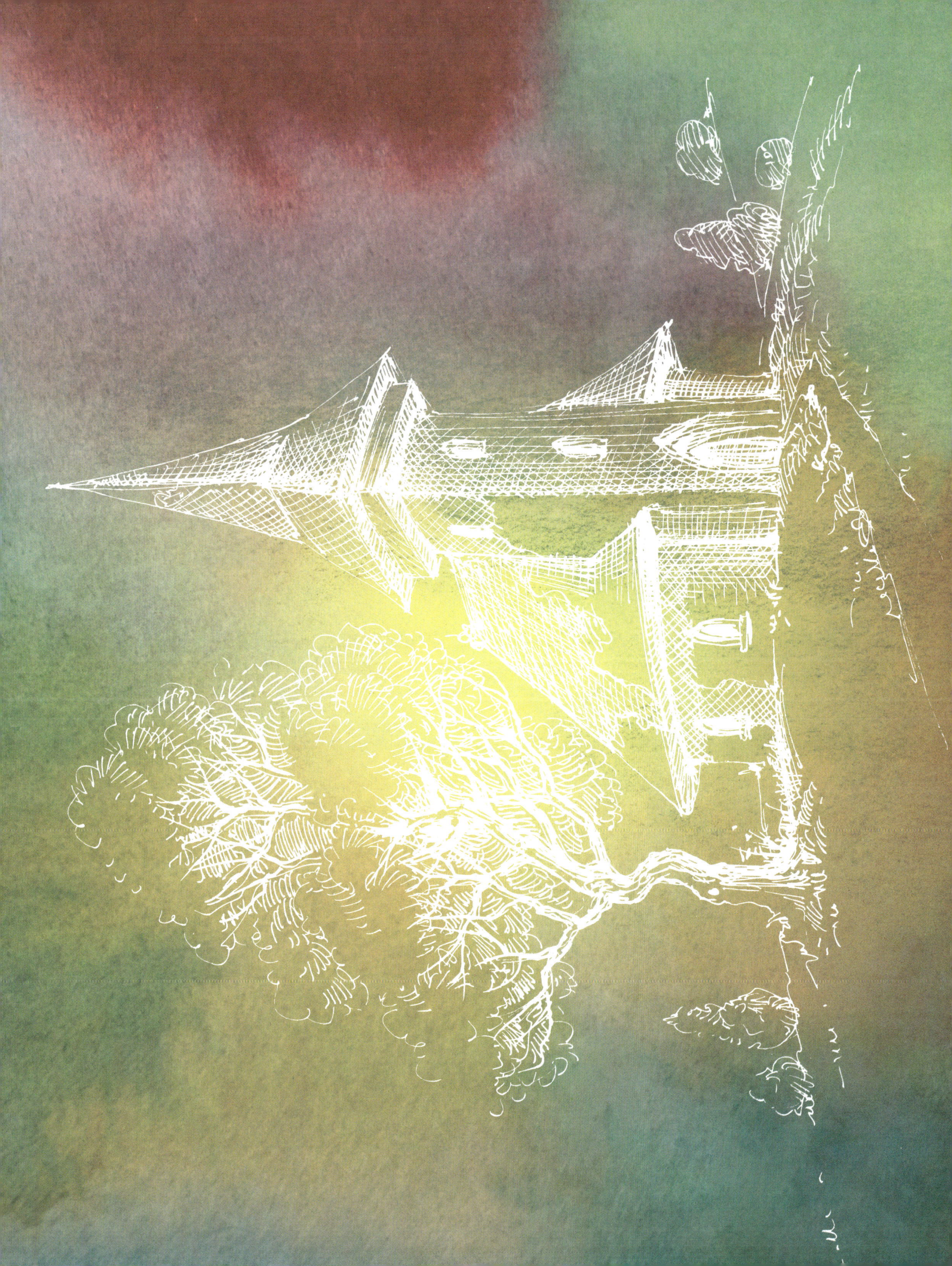

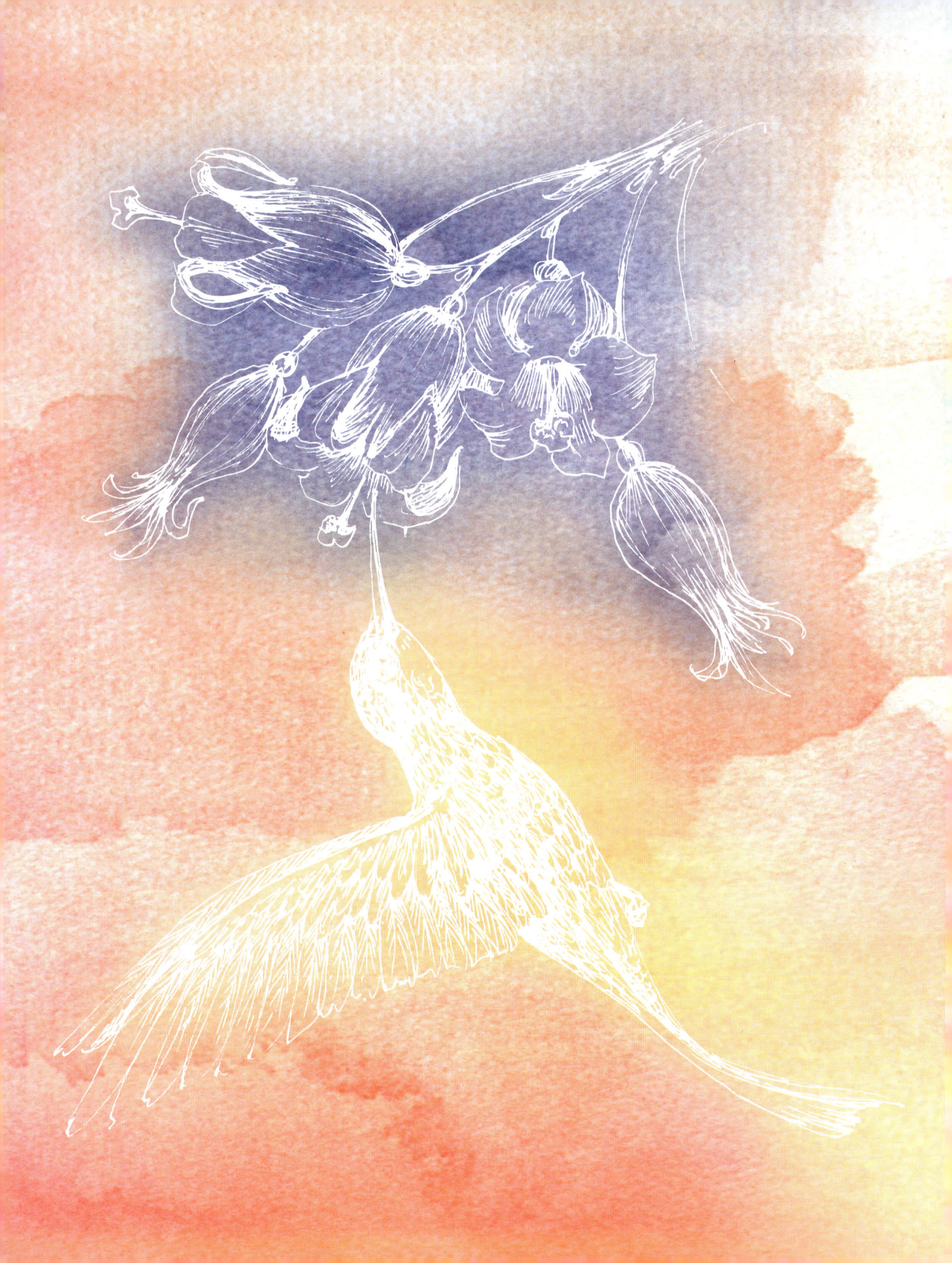

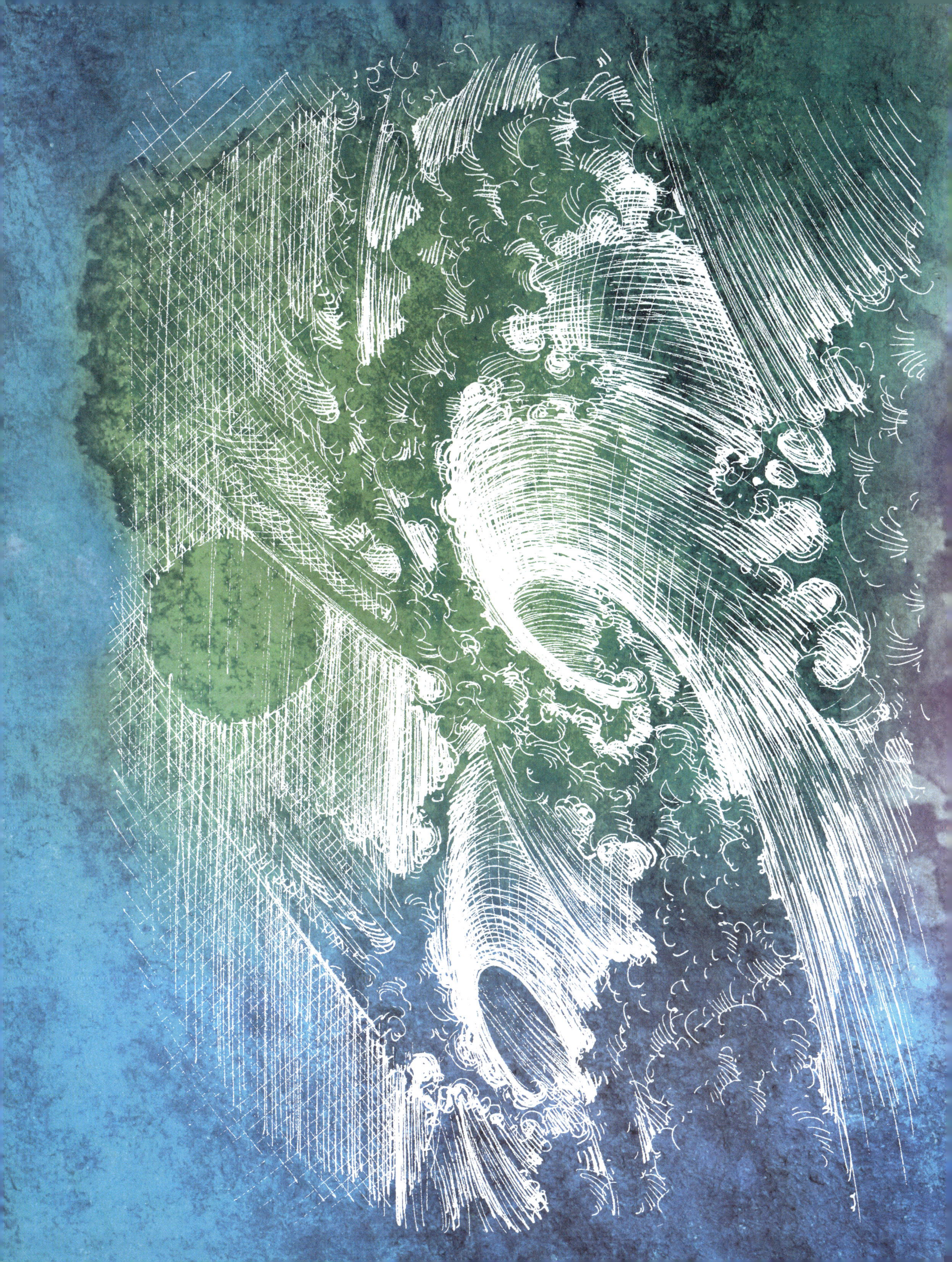

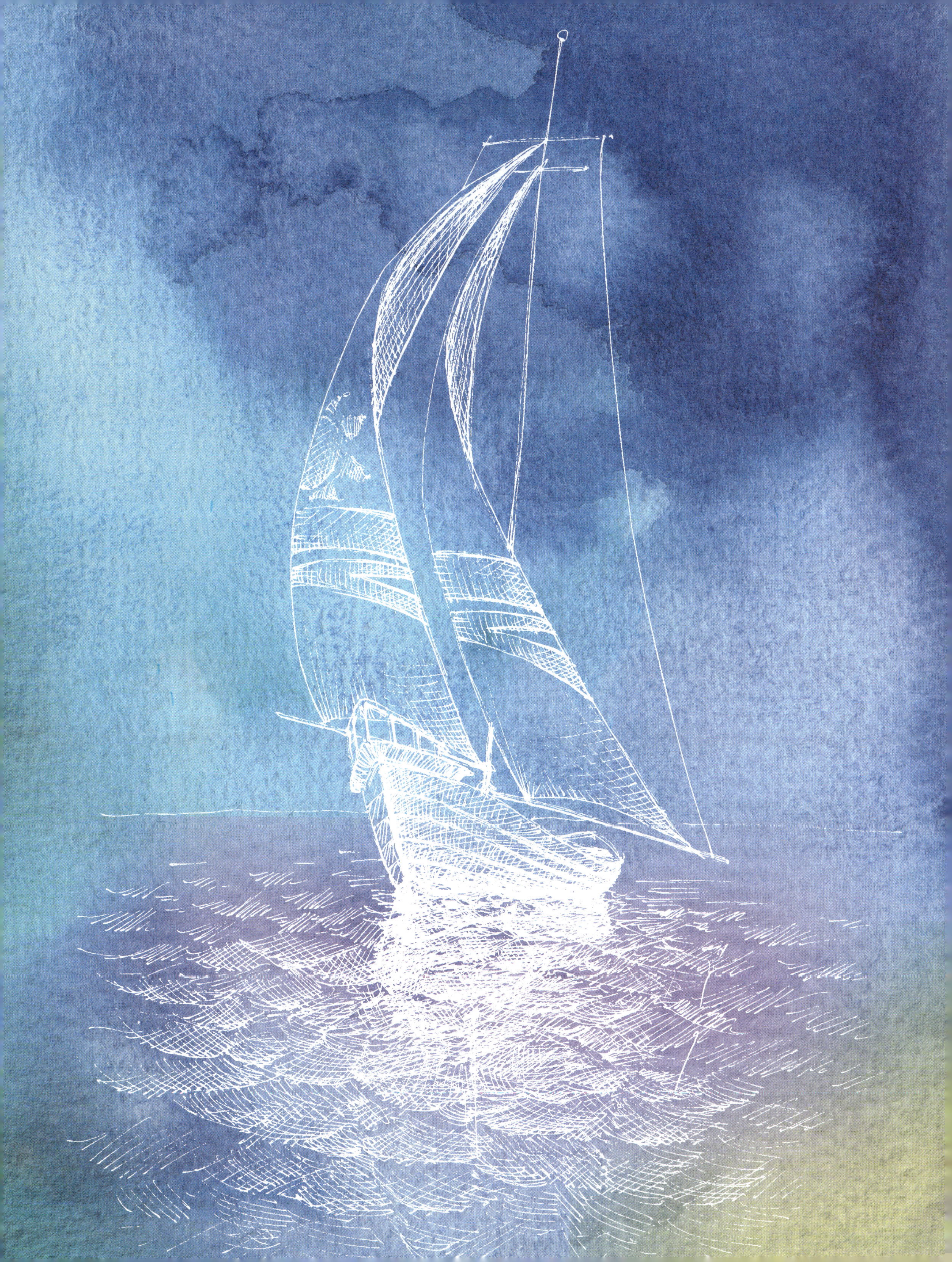

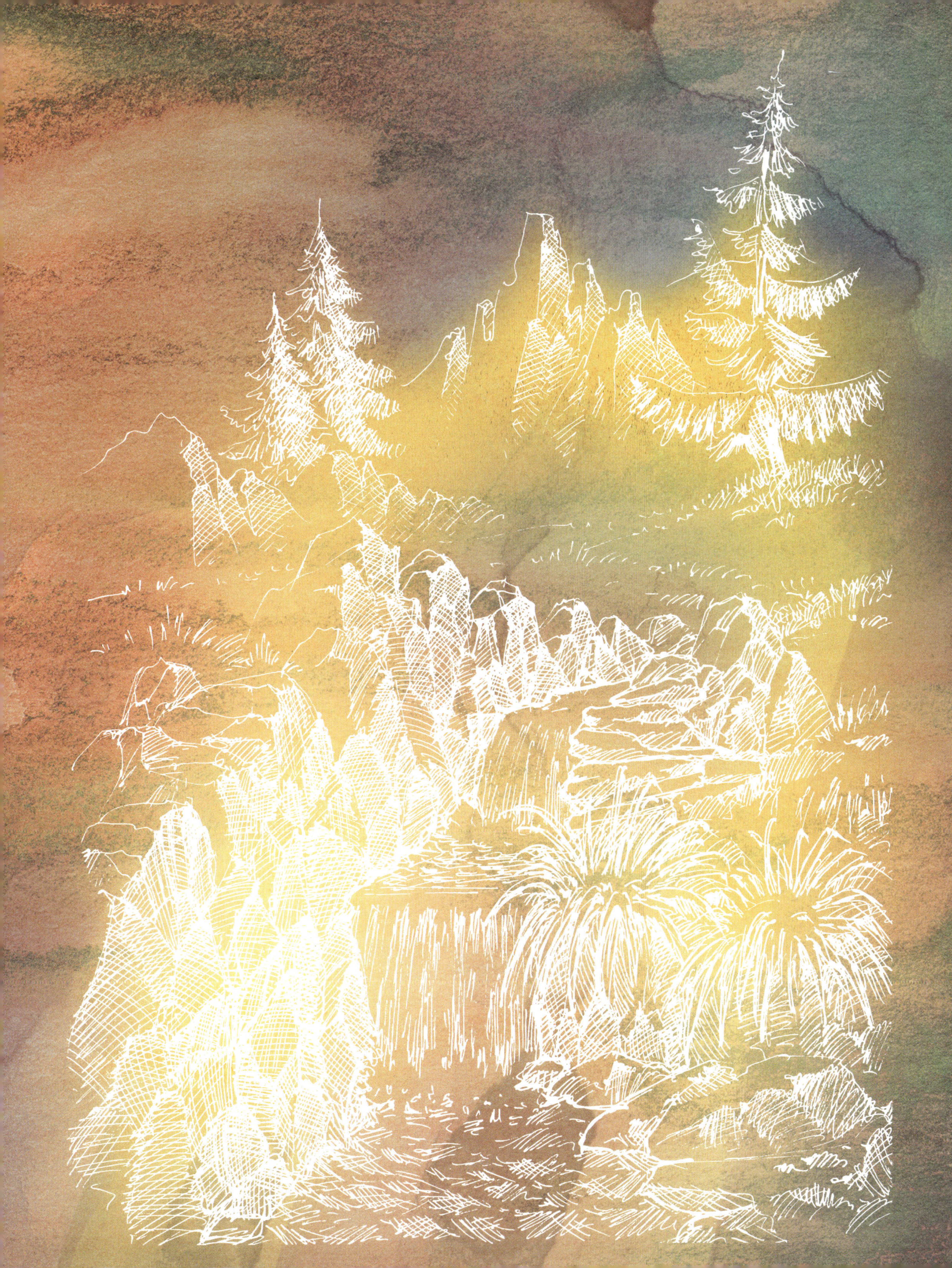

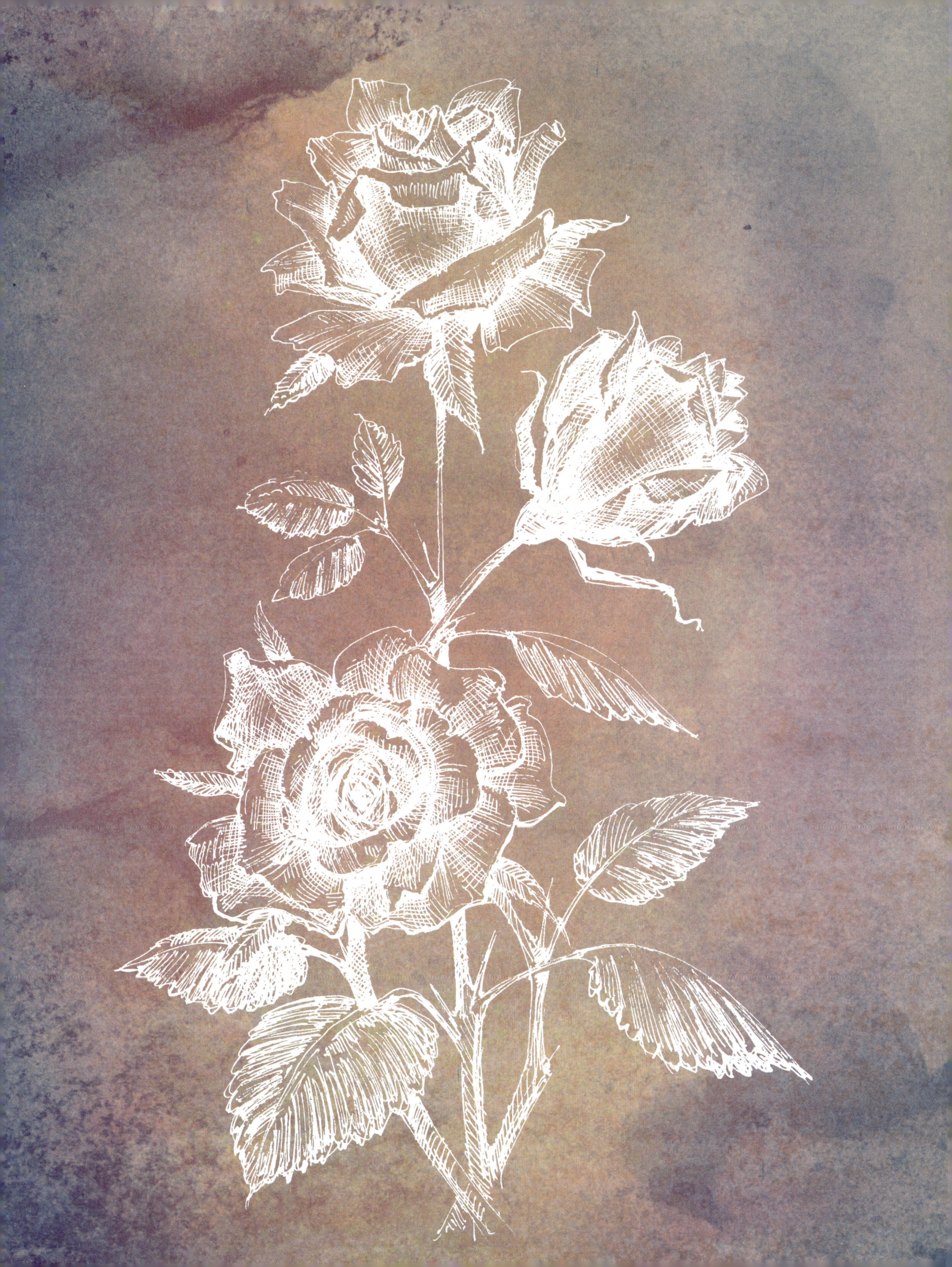

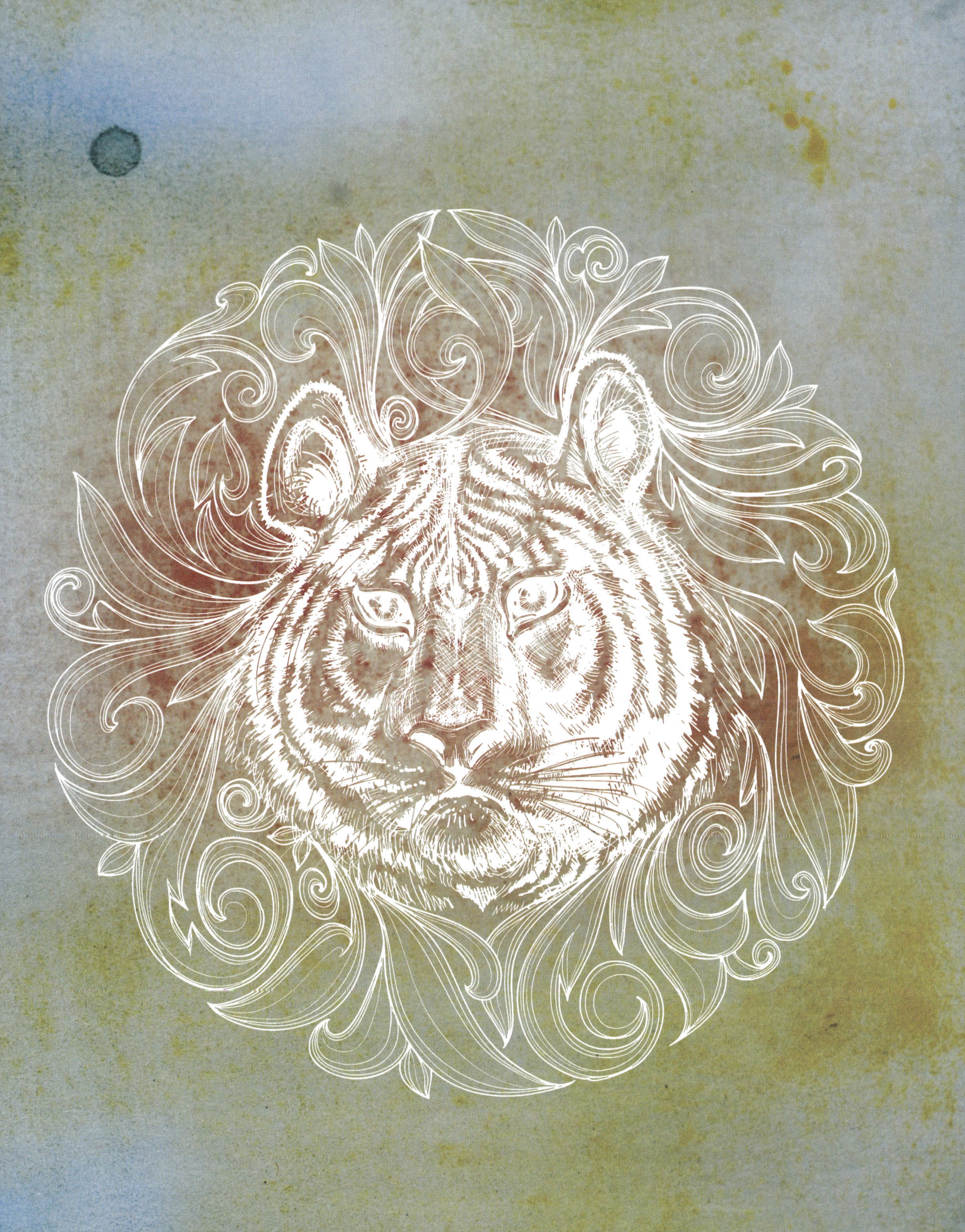